The
Apocalyptic
VISION
and the
Neutering *of*
ADVENTISM

The
Apocalyptic
VISION
and the
Neutering *of*
ADVENTISM

George R. Knight

R
REVIEW AND HERALD® PUBLISHING ASSOCIATION
Since 1861 | www.reviewandherald.com

This book was
Edited by Gerald Wheeler
Designed by Trent Truman
Cover art image of pencil: ©123rf.com/Iofoto
Interior designed by Tina M. Ivany
Typeset: Bembo 11/13

PRINTED IN U.S.A.
12   11   10   09   08   6   5   4   3   2

Library of Congress Cataloging-in-Publication Data
Knight, George R.
  The apocalyptic vision and the neutering of adventism / George R. Knight.
    p. cm.
  ISBN 978-0-8280-2385-6
  1. Seventh-Day Adventists—Doctrines. 2. Adventists—Doctrines. 3. Bible—Prophecies.
4. Christianity—Forecasting. I. Title.
  BX6154.K55 2008
  286.7—dc22

                                    2008029003

ISBN 978-0-8280-2385-6

Contents

Thoughts on the Word "Neutering" 6

Chapter 1 Enough of Beastly Preaching and
an Introduction to Neutering 7

Chapter 2 Another Look at Apocalyptic Prophecy
and Adventist History 28

Chapter 3 But Don't Forget the Beasts
(Including the Modern Ones)
and My Problem With Apocalyptic 52

Chapter 4 The Fallacy of Straight-line Thinking
and a Most Remarkable Prophecy 80

Chapter 5 Living the Apocalyptic Vision in the
Twenty-first Century 90

Chapter 6 A Glimpse of Neoapocalyptic
and a Belated Foreword 104

Thoughts on the Word "Neutering"

- "Neutering" is not a nice word.

- Neither is the process agreeable, whether it be physically or spiritually.

- Some will hate the metaphor,

    Others will love it,

        But *none will forget it.*

- If so, I have achieved the first part of my purpose in writing this brief book.

Chapter 1

Enough of Beastly Preaching and an Introduction to Neutering

Why be Adventist?

Good question. One I have struggled with during the past five decades.

For some of you the answer is simple. You can't help it. You were born that way.

For others it's an addiction. For one reason or another it "feels good" to be Adventist. You wouldn't know what to do with your lives without it.

But for me it is a serious problem. You see, I wasn't born that way. And after 47 years in the church I'm still not addicted.

There have to be good reasons for me to be an Adventist—or even remain one.

Reflecting on the Meaning of Adventism

The roots of my perspective go back to my childhood. Not only was I not born Adventist, but I didn't even profess Christianity for my first 19 years.

My cue for religion came from my father, who proclaimed that "all Christians are hypocrites" and who held with Freud that only weak people need to lean on God as a father figure. In my early-adult years he told me that his great failure in life was that all four of his children had become Christians. He has mellowed with age, but his earlier perspective shaped my own on the topic of religion.

My agnosticism came to a sudden halt at a series of evangelistic meetings in Eureka, California, in 1961. Just before I turned 20 I was baptized into the Seventh-day Adventist Church. And like many new converts, I took a good long look at you Adventists and your preachers. I soon came to one solid conclusion: *What a mess!* None of you were perfect, and I knew why. You obviously hadn't tried hard enough.

I still vividly remember promising God that I would be the first perfect Christian since Jesus. *No problem*, thought I. After all, I had boundless energy and barrels of determination. And then again, I hadn't found it all that difficult to be bad. And wasn't being good just as easy in the other direction?

Well, it wasn't. By 1969 I had three academic degrees in Adventist theology and was serving the church as a pastor. But things weren't going well. In fact, after nearly eight years of struggle I was as messed up as ever. And so were the churches I served.

One March morning I took out my ministerial credentials and put them in an envelope with a note to my conference president, resigning from the ministry.

Now, my conference president was a gracious man who wanted to "save me for the work." So he returned my credentials with a note of encouragement. He thought I was having a bad day. But I was having a bad life! All I wanted was out—out of both Adventism and Christianity. My only desire was to return to the happy hedonism I had enjoyed during my earlier years. So I again put my credentials in an envelope and sent them off a second time.

At that point the good man asked me to visit him at his home, where he prayed with me and for me and returned my credentials. But to no avail. I returned home, wrote a rather pointed letter as to what he could do with my credentials, and mailed the whole mess off a third time.

It was my first literary success. I never saw my credentials again. For the next six years I did not read my Bible, for six years I did not pray, for six years I wandered spiritually in a "far country" (Luke 15:13).

During those long years I studied philosophy for my doctorate. But by the time I received my degree I had concluded that philosophy was bankrupt in terms of answers to life's most basic questions. And that was important, since I had entered my studies hoping to find the "real meaning" of life that had eluded me in my Adventist experience.

About that time my major professor, an agnostic existentialist of Jewish heritage, told me one day that if he wasn't a Jew he'd be a nobody.

That statement from a man who routinely smashed religion in class caught me off guard. "What do you mean?" I asked. Josh's answer was as pointed as it was memorable. I still recall his passion as he proclaimed that it was his Jewishness that gave him meaning—that he wasn't just one of those millions of people out there, but a member of the community. The community, in fact, not only provided orientation for his life, but sent him all over the world as a speaker.

As he talked I reeled in astonishment, thinking to myself that Josh wasn't a Jew but an Adventist. (Of course, with a different background I could have substituted Baptist, Methodist, or Catholic.)

Josh helped me see what I should have discovered from Matthew 13 about the various plants and fish existing in every religious community until the harvest (verses 30, 49). He had enabled me to grasp the fact that all religious communities consist of two sorts of members—believers and cultural adherents. In Josh's case the most important thing about his religious orientation was that he had been born that way and raised in the community. His religious orientation was his life, even though he wasn't a "believer." It was his history, his culture, his social location, and he loved and respected it for all of those reasons.

Reflecting on my conversation with Josh many years later, I realized that if I had been born Adventist and if my father had been a pastor, my mother a church school teacher, and my grandfather a conference president, the most difficult and radical thing I could do would be to leave the church that had provided social meaning to my life. It would be easier to stay in rather than depart, even if I didn't believe. In fact, in such a circumstance becoming a pastor, administrator, or Bible teacher would be preferable to cutting off my cultural roots and family. After all, you don't have to believe that stuff. There is a certain level of comfort and security in "playing church." I could finally see how Josh had arrived at his destination, even though my own experience meant an uprooting from job, friends, and family when I accepted Adventism.

> *You don't have to believe that stuff. There is a certain level of comfort and security in "playing church."*

About the same time that Josh helped me to grasp the difference between cultural adherents and believers, a very bad thing happened to me, something that I never wanted to take place. My first Bible teacher "got invited" to my house for lunch. It wasn't my idea, but I couldn't get out of it.

It was a long day because I realized that he knew my spiritual condition. But he didn't preach a sermon to me, counsel me, or condemn me. He merely exuded an atmosphere of calm assurance in his faith and treated me with kindness and love. That day I met Jesus in the person of Robert W. Olson. When he left, I told my wife that he had what I needed.

That day, 14 years after I had become an Adventist, I became a

Christian. To put it another way, my Adventism got baptized. At that point I became spiritually active in Adventism again. It wasn't because Adventism's theology was perfect that I reconnected, but because its theology was closer to the Bible than that of any other church that I was aware of. In short, I was and am an Adventist by conviction rather than by choice.

My meandering journey might help readers understand why I used to be able to preach a sermon entitled "Why I Don't Like Adventists." And I really don't, but I finally stopped presenting it because it sounded a wee bit negative. Of course, I had no problem if they were Christian as well as Adventist. But if they were *only* Adventist, let me loose. You see, I once met a Seventh-day Adventist who was meaner than the devil. In fact, I once even met a vegan who was as vicious as the devil. To have any value, our Adventism must be immersed in Christianity. Without that immersion, it is no better than any other deluded "ism."

Not long ago I saw a bumper sticker that spoke to the point. "JESUS SAVE ME" read the large print. "From your people" declared the small. I thought the entire blurb might make a meaningful book title. And then there was the atheistic philosopher Friedrich Nietzsche, who proclaimed the profound truth of my early years: "The best argument against Christianity is Christians." In all too many cases the same dictum would hold for the best argument against Adventism.

Well, as you can see, my mind wanders in strange directions. But the upshot of my journey has left me with three inescapable questions that have driven my life both existentially and intellectually.

What is the meaning of life both personally and universally?

Why be a Christian?

Why be a Seventh-day Adventist?

I have to admit that I am not happy with most people's (including most Adventists') answers to those all-important questions. But it's time to move beyond biography to more important issues.

Adventist or Merely Evangelical?

Early in 2007 I presented a paper entitled "The Missiological Roots of Adventist Higher Education and the Ongoing Tension Between Adventist Mission and Academic Vision"[1] to a group of Seventh-day Adventist educational leaders and the church administrators who chair their boards. The content of my talk dealt with the necessary and ongoing tension and balance between what academics might want to see in higher education and the missiological goals of the denomination. The paper also focused on the balance between general Christian and specifically Adventist concerns.

In the question-and-answer session that followed I made the point that if Adventism loses its apocalyptic vision, it has lost its reason for existing as either a church or as a system of education.

In response, one administrator quite aggressively stated that what we needed was to get rid of apocalyptic and preach the gospel. I tried to suggest that rightly understood, apocalyptic is gospel. But he had his own views on the topic. Getting a bit excited, he pointed out that his institution was growing rapidly by emphasizing the gospel without apocalyptic. He apparently saw little connection between the two realms.

Looking back, I have wondered if he had earlier been a victim of what I will later in this chapter call beastly apocalyptic preaching or had suffered from overexposure to the ad-nauseam bickering by some Adventists over apocalyptic minutia. But he was a successful, pragmatic administrator whose nontraditional institution enrolling largely non-Adventist students was growing rapidly in spite of its lack of Adventist focus.

If Seventh-day Adventist institutions are Christian only in the sense that they have Jesus and the evangelical gospel, then any good evangelical school will do. And with that one stroke we have removed any compelling reason for Seventh-day Adventist schools to exist.

The next day in an unrelated discussion someone made the point that more and more well-heeled, highly educated Adventist parents are sending their children to non-Adventist institutions. All admitted to that truth. But why, and what could be done about it? became the focal point of discussion.

I don't think it was explicitly stated, but part of the answer is obvious. If Seventh-day Adventist institutions are Christian only in the sense that they have Jesus and the evangelical gospel, then any good evangelical school will do. And with that one stroke we have removed any compelling reason for Seventh-day Adventist schools to exist. Even though they might be good institutions, no one can say that they are necessary ones. There is a difference between being a good school and having distinctive importance as an institution.

A few days after the conference I received an interesting letter from a participant in the meetings, who wrote that "I do understand rather well where [Dr. X] is coming from, having grown up in the era of fear mongering about the 'time of the end' and legalistic interpretations about how to arrive at a state where one no longer sinned (which my father and many others believed was necessary to attain so that they could 'stand without a Mediator' during the time of trouble), and hearing a number of older people despair that they could ever be 'good enough for God to love me' . . .

Why have a Seventh-day Adventist Church? What function or use does it have? Is it important or even necessary? Is it merely another denomination that turns out to be a bit stranger than some of the others because of its "hang-up" with the seventh day and certain dietary issues?

in contrast to a more Christ-centered philosophy. However, this is a pretty radical swing of the pendulum, to dump our heritage and beliefs in eschatology/last-day events, along with the implications of our historical stance on [the] . . . prophecies, and focus only on being Christlike. So then what would be our excuse for existing as a unique denomination, and operating a school system? Granted we still have the Sabbath [and] state of the dead . . . , but if we find a group that keeps the seventh day . . . , we could join up with them (Seventh Day Baptists, anyone?) and feel perfectly at home. . . . Obviously, we'd have to downplay references that describe Ellen White as 'inspired,' since so much of her writings deal with last-day events. But just make her over into a 'devotional writer' and no problem!

"But why does [Dr. X] view being Christlike and holding to traditional eschatological views as being mutually exclusive?

"This whole argument is absolutely at the core of defining who we are and where we are going and deserves to be laid out in fairly stark terms in a manner that can stimulate thought and discussion in the context of Adventist . . . mission."

Such thoughts bring us to the frontier of the issue of Why have a Seventh-day Adventist Church? What function or use does it have? Is it important or even necessary? Is it merely another denomination that turns out to be a bit stranger than some of the others because of its "hang-up" with the seventh day and certain dietary issues?

Such questions raise complex issues related to the nature of Adventism and the proper balance between those aspects of our belief system that make us Christian and those that make us Adventist and how they fit together. Thoughtful people can hardly avoid such topics. In actuality, they ought to stand at the center of discussion.

As I have sought to demonstrate in such books as *A Search for Identity*, the struggle for a balanced Adventism has been at the center of the historical development of Seventh-day Adventist theology.[2] Over time we have oscillated between overemphasizing those aspects of our belief system that make us Christian and those that distinguish us as distinctively Adventist. Today we have in the church what I call the Adventist Adventists, who see everything the denomination teaches to be uniquely Adventist and groan a bit when we call ourselves evangelical. On the other extreme are those Adventists that we can describe as Christian Christians. Those at that pole of the denomination are overjoyed to be evangelical and shy away from Ellen White, the eschatological implications of the Sabbath, the heavenly sanctuary, and so on. Fortunately, in the middle we find some who might be styled as Christian Adventists, whose Adventism finds meaning in the evangelical framework that we share with other Christians.

Put in a different way, there was a time that Ellen White noted that some Adventists had been at work on the law until they had gotten to be as dry as the hills of Gilboa. Today she might say something similar about those who have focused on grace so much that they have lost sight of the law altogether. Balance is the goal, but clearly that is something difficult to discover and almost impossible to maintain in an unbalanced world. Yet that doesn't mean that we shouldn't seek to approximate it in our ministries.

The Problematic Jesus

Before I go any further, I need to point out the obvious truth that Jesus of Nazareth was not politically correct in His statements. He not only declared that there was truth and that He had the truth, but that He was *the* truth, *the* way, and *the* life, and that no one could come to the Father except by Him (John 14:6).

Jesus stood for something. Beyond that, He believed that there was error—that some people and ideas were just plain wrong.

As one who unabashedly and aggressively stood for something, Jesus would not fit well into our twenty-first-century culture (including many of our churches). Calling people, especially respected religious and intellectual leaders, hypocrites and whitewashed sepulchres full of dead men's bones is plainly not acceptable.

But making problematic statements was not Jesus' only difficulty. He was also affected with what we might call "sanctified arrogance." He so believed in Himself and His politically incorrect message that He told 12 relatively unlearned men to spread it to the entire world. That commission staggers the normal imagination. Who did He think He was? And who did they think they were? *But they did it!*

Now, you don't do those kinds of things without some firm convictions. You don't give your life and your worldly goods without *knowing* that you have the truth. If Jesus had been politically correct and had lacked sanctified arrogance, Christianity would have existed for a few years as a backwater Jewish sect and then blended back into the Near Eastern woodwork.

Early Adventism suffered largely from the same "cultural defects" that Jesus did. It believed that it had *the* truth or *present* truth for its day. And it came to believe that it had a mission to all the world in spite of its smallness.

If Jesus had been politically correct and had lacked sanctified arrogance, Christianity would have existed for a few years as a backwater Jewish sect and then blended back into the Near Eastern woodwork.

Early in the twentieth century the large Protestant denominations, realizing that the mission field was just too big, decided to divide up certain areas of the world among the Anglicans, Methodists, Presbyterians, and so on. But the Adventists wanted no part of such a commonsense approach. They rejected the logic and claimed the whole world as their sphere of influence. Although a little people, they had big ideas. Why? Because they were impelled by an apocalyptic vision straight out of the heart of the book of Revelation that they believed all the world needed to hear. The Adventists notified the other denominations that they could divide things up, but that Adventists saw every nation as their mission field.

Talk about sanctified arrogance! *But they did it.* Through dedicating lives and sacrificing means Adventism became the most widespread unified Protestant group in the history of Christianity. But undergirding that success were some politically incorrect understandings regarding *truth* and a sanctified arrogance that reflected on the shortcomings of other branches of Christianity and the importance of God's last-day message.

I think of the sacrifices of my wife's family. The Bond brothers gave their lives to establish Adventism in Spain. One would lay his bones there, a victim of poisoning, while her grandfather was at times stoned and driven from village to village. He also died an early death. Why? Why did they go? Why did they give all?

On a broader scale, why should any of us risk our life for a cause? Why live for it? Why did those early Adventists sacrifice their means and their children to mission? Only because of a deep conviction that they had a message right out of the heart of the book of Revelation that all the world needed to hear before Jesus returns in the clouds of heaven.

An Introduction to Neutering

But the "good news" is that Adventism in the early twenty-first century, especially in developed nations, has largely moved beyond such "primitive" and unsophisticated ideas. We have "gotten the victory" over standing too vigorously for the denomination's traditional perspective. Rich and increased with politically correct assumptions, we have lost that sanctified arrogance that made us believe that we had a message that the whole world *must* hear.

> *Why did those early Adventists sacrifice their means and their children to mission? Only because of a deep conviction that they had a message right out of the heart of the book of Revelation that all the world needed to hear before Jesus returns in the clouds of heaven.*

The results? Shrinkage in the North American Division (and other developed world sectors of the church) in all four major groups—White, Black, Asian, and Hispanic. While the overall number of members is increasing, that growth is from immigration. A case in point is the fact that both the "White" and "regional" conferences in New York City are nearly entirely populated by members of Caribbean heritage. We are largely failing in reaching native-born Whites and Blacks in that great city, and in most other parts of the developed nations. The composition of the church in Great Britain and much of Europe indicates the same pattern.

Part of the problem is that Adventism has to a large extent lost the apocalyptic foundation of its message. Some years ago I attended a symposium of Seventh-day Adventist religion scholars who addressed the issue of why they personally were Seventh-day Adventists. It was a group of presenters from across the theological spectrum, and all were very sincere in their beliefs. But their testimonies, from my perspective, shot wide of the mark. The reasons largely centered on cultural and relationship issues and the way they had been nurtured from childhood into the community—a lot of the warm fuzzies of religion.

That is OK for insiders, I thought, but as an outsider to the club of the born-in-the-church community I saw absolutely no reason to become Seventh-day Adventist from what I heard. I could find all of those things elsewhere—and often better and cheaper. After all, one tenth of my money and one seventh of my time are pretty steep dues.

> *When a church becomes politically correct in all its claims and when it loses a proper amount of sanctified arrogance regarding its message and mission, it manages to neuter itself, even if it continues to brag about its potency.*

I personally saw nothing of a magnitude that would have led me to become an Adventist if I hadn't been one already and certainly nothing to die for or even give my life for in sacrificial service. But since I was being politically correct I kept my mouth shut and let everyone enjoy their warm fuzzies—or what I thought were relatively meaningless fuzzies—in terms of the significance of Adventism.

Meanwhile, I was wondering to myself why I personally should be a Seventh-day Adventist. *If that's all there is to it,* I remember thinking, *then there is no really good reason to be an Adventist unless you were born that way or are so socially and culturally impoverished that you lack other satisfying alternatives.*

Put more bluntly, when a church becomes politically correct in all its claims and when it loses a *proper* amount of sanctified arrogance regarding its message and mission, it manages to neuter itself, even if it continues to brag about its potency.

Do you understand the concept of neutering? I must admit that I am a bit ignorant on the fine points of the project. I am neither a neuteree nor a neuterer, but I think I have the basic idea.

Neutering and even self-neutering have a long history in the biblical world and, you will be glad to know, even in Adventism. Daniel, for example, had probably suffered the operation. Potiphar, as a functionary of Pharaoh's court, may also have fit into that category, which might help explain some of his wife's actions.

Jesus noted that "there are eunuchs who have been so from birth, and there are eunuchs who have been made eunuchs by men, and there are eunuchs who have made themselves eunuchs for the sake of the kingdom of heaven" (Matt. 19:12). Origen, the famous third-century theologian, read that text, and out came the knife. He neutered himself for the kingdom. In the made-so-by-others category are some of the choirboys of the Middle Ages. The operation apparently kept their voices higher. Every time I read such accounts I am thankful I live in the twenty-first century and can't carry a tune.

The good news is that we Seventh-day Adventists have also provided our own candidate for the neutering hall of fame. Walter Harper, a colporteur, eradicated a certain realm of temptation by the process, but then went on to marry twice, with both wives knowing the problem beforehand. The situation led to some interesting counsel from Ellen White. Meanwhile, some years ago I met a man who told me that his grandfather was Walter Harper. He was absolutely shocked that I knew who his grandfather was. As you might expect, I was a bit more than shocked myself. It came out in conversation that he was really a step grandson. That piece of information helped me sleep better that night.

Now, as noted above, I'm not certain about all the implications of neutering, but they tell me that it does seem to be one of the more effective ways to stem the tide of productivity.

The best example of religious neutering in the modern world is Protestant liberalism, which by the 1920s had divested itself of such "primitive" ideas as the virgin birth, Christ's resurrection, the substitutionary atonement, miracles, the Second Advent, creationism, and, of course, a divinely inspired Bible in the sense that it had information from beyond the human realm that could be obtained from no other source but divine revelation.

Human reason came to the fore as the source of knowledge, doctrine became unimportant if not distasteful, and Jesus morphed from being a Savior who died in our place to being the best of good people and an example worthy of emulation. In the process, Christianity largely shifted from the realm of religion to that of ethics.

With those masterstrokes of the human intellect, Protestant liberalism effectively lost its distinctive Christian message. Or, to put it more bluntly, it had neutered itself.

The *eventual* result was shrinkage by the millions in America's mainline denominations. Between 1965 and the early 1990s, for example, Presbyterian membership plummeted from 4.2 million to 2.8 million members, a 34 percent drop. During the same period Methodism went from 11 to 8.7 million, Episcopalianism from 3.6 to 2.4 million, and the Disciples of Christ from 2 to 1 million—21 percent, 34 percent, and 50 percent declines, respectively.[3]

Beyond shrinkage, mainline average membership age shot up, and, of course, morale plummeted. *Newsweek* blandly reported that "the mainline denominations may be dying because they lost their theological integrity." Duke Divinity School's Stanley Hauerwas put it more colorfully when he claimed that "God is killing mainline Protestantism in America and we [blankety-blank] well deserve it."[4]

People are looking for a church that stands over against culture, one that is arrogant enough to believe that there is truth and error and that it has the truth.

The mainline disaster spawned a number of influential books on the topic. In *The Empty Church: The Suicide of Liberal Christianity* Thomas C. Reeves suggests that the only hope for the mainline is to recover orthodox theology, including a faith in an all-powerful God who was and is capable of the miraculous.[5]

Then there is Wade Clark Roof and William McKinney's *American Mainline Religion*, with its prediction of the continuing shrinkage of liberal Christianity even if it manages to find some sense of theological meaning.[6] And Roger Finke and Rodney Stark's *The Churching of America, 1776-1990: Winners and Losers in Our Religious Economy* argues the outrageous thesis that "*religious organizations are stronger to the degree that they impose significant costs in terms of sacrifice and even stigma upon their members.* . . . People tend to value religion on the basis of how costly it is to belong—the more one must sacrifice in order to be in good standing, the more valuable the religion."[7]

Then, of course, we have the granddaddy of the study of the slow death of liberalism, Dean Kelley's *Why Conservative Churches Are Growing*. Kelley (a United Methodist) is quite up front with the answers. *The conservative churches are growing because they stand for something.* If, he suggests, people are going to join a church at all, it is because it represents a special truth and knows it. That is, people are looking for a church that stands over against culture, one that is arrogant enough to believe that there is truth and error and that it has the truth.[8]

If there is no such special truth, why join? In fact, Kelley points out, in the case of liberal Protestantism, which by the 1970s had become merely a part of a middle-of-the-road American population, why not leave? And not finding sufficient reason for remaining, large numbers of people made sense out of their lives by exiting the mainline denominations. The same could be said today of many Adventists.

The key word for liberal Protestantism by the 1960s had been "relevance." They sought to be relevant to their culture. What they proved, however, was that the shortest road to irrelevance is *mere* relevance. After all, who needs more of what can be found in the larger culture?

Adventism became strong by proclaiming that it had a prophetic message for our time. And it is that message repackaged for the twenty-first century that will give Adventism strength both in the present and the future.

Now, there is nothing wrong with being relevant from a biblical perspective, but to be *merely* relevant is the path to being acculturated or absorbed into the larger culture. A healthy Christianity must of necessity stand over against the values of the larger culture and hold truths that the surrounding culture finds distasteful. Perhaps history's most well-known countercultural document is the Sermon on the Mount. Its value system is a radical departure from that of the larger world and that of most churches.

Having said all those things, we should add that irrelevance is not the answer. We as Christians should be standing for things that are not only true but also important for the times in which we live. And it is at that point that Adventism can make a contribution. It became strong by proclaiming that it had a prophetic message for our time. And it is that message repackaged for the twenty-first century that will give Adventism strength in both the present and the future.

On the other hand, if we discover that Adventism does not have something unique and valuable to offer, let's be honest, fold up our tents, and find something useful to do with our lives. *Adventism cannot escape the dilemma between being meaningful or being neutered. It can't have both.*

The Neutering of Adventism

Those thoughts bring me to the neutering of Adventism. Modern

Adventism, whether it likes it or not, is firmly rooted in the apocalyptic visions of Daniel and Revelation. As I look at those Bible books I see at least three ways that the movement can neuter itself. And, believe it or not, we Adventists have found all of them.

The first is "beastly preaching." We have endured too much of that slant on the apocalypse. As I remember my own coming into the church, I realize that I knew all about the beasts but not too much about the Lord of the beasts. The beasts and the time prophecies have their place, but too much of even a good thing can turn out to be beastly. It is all too easy for us Adventist types to get off onto the fine points of apocalyptic while forgetting the *One* who makes it meaningful.

Ellen White points to the center when she writes that "the sacrifice of Christ as an atonement for sin is the great truth around which all other truths cluster. In order to be rightly understood and appreciated, every truth in the Word of God, from Genesis to Revelation, must be studied in the light that streams from the cross of Calvary. . . . The Son of God uplifted on the cross. This is to be the foundation of every discourse given by our ministers."[8]

> *Gospel evangelism is to get people maladjusted to a culture that stands judged by the cross and found wanting.*

I must admit to having done my own share of beastly preaching. But I early learned that if I couldn't genuinely root my message in the love of God and the cross of Christ I didn't have a Christian message. It was only beastly preaching, no matter how valid the topic, without that all-important integration.

But, we need to note, both the cross of Christ and the love of God are countercultural in a world featuring "me" and "getting." Yet I have heard some Adventist leaders in one part of the world advocating the role of evangelism as that of getting people adjusted to culture.

No! was my reply. Gospel evangelism is to get people maladjusted to a culture that stands judged by the cross and found wanting; maladjusted to a culture that calls violence and illicit sex entertainment; maladjusted to a culture that pays tens of millions to ballplayers but puts elementary teachers on a starvation wage.

As alluded to earlier, even such basic Christian virtues as loving one's enemies and rewarding the meek are countercultural. Such activities are not normal. Let's face it, *Christianity is an abnormal religion. God wants us to be abnormal by this world's standards.*

While thinking of the centrality of Christ and His life, death, and resurrection, we need not avoid the apocalyptic. To the contrary, Christ is the centerfold of the apocalypse in both Daniel and Revelation. In Revelation, for example:

He is the Alpha and Omega, the one who has victory over death and holds the keys to death and the grave (Rev. 1:18).

- In chapters 1–3 He is the Lord of the church, wandering among the lampstands.
- In chapters 4 and 5 He is the Lamb found worthy because He shed His blood to ransom humans, and He is the Lion of the tribe of Judah.
- In Revelation 6 He is the Lamb opening the seven seals.
- In chapter 12 He is the Babe who grew up to be the Lamb who conquers the dragon through His blood.
- Chapter 14 pictures Him as the one coming in the clouds of heaven to reap the harvest.
- And in chapter 19 He is the King of kings and Lord of lords arriving on a white horse to bring salvation to His followers.

The first route to the neutering of Adventism in the Apocalypse is beastly preaching—preaching that fails to put Christ and the love of God at the center of every message.

In summary, let me repeat that the first route to the neutering of Adventism in the Apocalypse is beastly preaching—preaching that fails to put Christ and the love of God at the center of every message. As we move toward a less beastly approach to apocalyptic we need to keep at the forefront of our thinking the truth that biblical preaching is not gospel versus apocalyptic but gospel *and* apocalyptic. Apocalyptic rightly understood is gospel. But even in the gospel we need proper balance. Without balance we have beastly preaching.

The second and third ways Adventists can neuter their message are both related to that Christ who is the center of John's Apocalypse. Revelation 5, in which the apostle encounters two figures, highlights both aspects:

In verse 5 he hears about the Lion of the tribe of Judah, who is able to open the scroll of world history.

But when he opens his eyes in verse 6 he sees a Lamb who had been slain.

Here we find a strange combination. Who has ever heard of a lamb that was also a lion?

We will return to that combination. But first we need to examine the second way in which Adventists can neuter their message—by removing the "lambishness" of the Lamb.

Please note the featured characteristic of the Lamb in Revelation 5:

1. Verse 6 describes it as one slain.
2. Verse 9 sets the Lamb forth as the slain one who ransomed people by His blood.
3. Verse 12 proclaims that He is worthy to receive honor because He was slain.

The same emphasis appears in Revelation 12:11, in which the saints are conquerors because of the blood of the Lamb, and in Revelation 1:5, which tells us that Christ has "freed us from our sins by his blood." Now one doesn't have to be a biblical genius to conclude with Ian Boxall that "though John does not spell out the mechanism by which this occurs, the reference to blood suggests sacrifice."[9]

Sacrifice is central to both testaments. In the Old Testament we find the Passover lamb, the lamb of the daily sacrifice, and the lambs and other animals slain for individual sins. All died in the place of sinners.

The New Testament brings that picture to the fore when John the Baptist cries out, "Behold, the Lamb of God, who takes away the sin of the world!" (John 1:29). And Paul proclaims to the Galatians that "Christ redeemed us from the curse of the law, having become a curse for us—for it is written, 'Cursed be every one who hangs on a tree'" (Gal. 3:13). He writes to the Corinthians that "Christ" is "our paschal lamb," who "has been sacrificed" (1 Cor. 5:7). Central to Paul's description of the gospel is the fact that "Christ died for our sins" (1 Cor. 15:3; cf. Isa. 53:5).

On the other hand, Paul also noted that the teaching of the sacrificed Lamb was the most disgusting aspect of Christianity—a stumbling block to Jews and foolishness to Gentiles (1 Cor. 1:23, 18).

We might as well face it—the message of Christ's sacrificial death on the cross is *not logical*. At the very least it sounds like utter foolishness to proclaim that the best of humans died so that a pack of criminals and rebels could get what they don't deserve (i.e., grace). However, while human reason may continue to caricature the Bible's clear teaching on the slain Lamb, such reason is not on a level with God's revelation in the Bible on the topic.[10]

What is important at this juncture is to note the repeated proclamation of the book of Revelation that it is *only* because of what Jesus did by shedding His blood on the cross *on our behalf* that positioned Him to be victor. As George Eldon Ladd put it, Christ's "worthiness is not based in particular on his deity, upon his relation to God, upon his incarnation, or his perfect human life, but upon his sacrificial death."[11] In short, the Lamb achieved victory by being slaughtered.

It is the Lamb slain for us that is the unique element in Christianity. Ellen White points out that human effort lies at the foundation of all other approaches to God.[12] By way of contrast, at the foundation and center of Christianity stands the Lamb who died on our behalf to put God's gift of grace on a firm basis.

The only thing Christianity has going for it is the Lamb of God who was slain *and whose blood paves the way for salvation through a method other than human effort.* Take away the Lamb who died on our behalf, and all you have is ethics.

I would like to suggest that *the only thing Christianity has going for it is the Lamb of God who was slain* and whose blood paves the way for salvation through a method other than human effort. *Take away the Lamb who died on our behalf, and all you have is ethics.*

Now, I have nothing against ethics and the good life, but without the slain Lamb there is no hope. Put more bluntly: ethics without the saving work of Christ for us equals death. That point is precisely where the 1920s liberals went off the track. *They neutered the Lamb and in the process neutered themselves.* At the very center of the Apocalypse of John stands the slain or slaughtered Lamb.

That brings us to the Lion of the tribe of Judah and the third way that we Adventists can neuter our message. But before proceeding any further, we need to examine the connection between the symbols of Lamb and Lion in Revelation. Outside of the fact that they both refer to Christ, the main thing that unites them is violence. In Revelation both are violent symbols: the Lamb because it is slaughtered and the Lion because of what it does. *We find the violence of the symbols of Lamb and Lion united in* the unlikely phrase *"the wrath of the Lamb"* (Rev. 6:16). Whoever heard of a wrathful lamb?

Wrath! Now, here is a nasty word that, coupled with violence, is politically incorrect and makes all of us good Adventists a bit nervous. I personally managed to avoid the word for two decades. But the sad truth is that just because we get rid of beastly preaching does not mean that we can be free of all difficult biblical topics.

And wrath is one topic that is impossible to dump. It may be unpopular with some theologians, but it is very popular with God. The number of Bible references to God's wrath exceeds 580, and the Revelation of John is not least in this matter. Writers have utilized barrels of ink to explain away God's wrath, but in the final analysis the Lion of the tribe of Judah will act to end the problem of sin.

Let's not go astray here. God's wrath is not an emotional anger comparable with human wrath. To the contrary, God's wrath is a function of His love. God hates the sin that continues to destroy the lives and happiness of His created beings. He is weary of dead babies, cancer, and blindness; rape, murder, and theft; holocausts, Rwandas, and Iraqs.

If all that Christianity has going for it is the slain Lamb, all that Adventism has going for it is the Lion of the tribe of Judah. An Adventism without the Lion is a neutered Adventism, just as a Christianity without the slaughtered Lamb is a neutered Christianity.

In His timing God will respond to the souls under the altar who cry out, "O Sovereign Lord. . . how long" before You put an end to the mess we call world history (Rev. 6:10)? As W. L. Walker puts it, God's "wrath only goes forth because God is love, and because sin is that which injures His children and is opposed to the purpose of His love."[13] And Alan Richardson points out that "only a certain kind of degenerate Protestant theology has attempted to contrast the wrath of God with the mercy of Christ."[14]

God, as the Bible pictures Him, cannot and will not forever stand idly by while His creation suffers. His reaction is judgment on that sin that is destroying His people, and we should see that judgment as the real meaning of biblical wrath. God condemns sin in judgment and will eventually act to eradicate it completely.

That is where the wrath of the Lamb comes in. That is where the Lion of the tribe of Judah enters, pictured in Revelation 19 as arriving from heaven on a white horse to put an end to the sin problem and its ongoing misery.

The plain fact is that if we have only the Lamb of God, we have only half a gospel. The Lamb has been slaughtered, yet God's children continue to suffer. The climactic phase of the Lamb's work is His function as the Lion of the tribe of Judah at the end of time. Thus the wrath of the Lamb.

The apocalypse is about the end of sin and a new heaven and a new earth. The apocalypse is what Adventism is all about. *If all that Christianity has going for it is the slain Lamb, all that Adventism has going for it is the Lion of the tribe of Judah. An Adventism without the Lion is a neutered Adventism, just as a Christianity without the slaughtered Lamb is a neutered Christianity.*

As Seventh-day Adventists God does not call us to be prophets of respectability but proclaimers of the message of the Lion and the Lamb.

And a serious message it is. That is where another unpopular word comes in—fear. "Fear God and give him glory," we read in Revelation 14:7, "for the hour of his judgment has come."

What a nasty thing to say about God. After all, announcing that people should "fear God" is politically incorrect in the early twenty-first century. "Certainly," we hear some saying, "fear means respect and reverence for God."

And so it does. But it also means fear in the sense of being afraid of the One who will not forever tolerate the sinful attitudes and actions that continue to destroy His children. It means fear in the sense of those who call "to the mountains and rocks, 'Fall on us and hide us from the face of him who is seated on the throne, and from the wrath of the Lamb; for the great day of their wrath has come, and who can stand before it?'" (Rev. 6:16, 17). How blind can we get if we limit fear to reverence and respect?

> **A neutered understanding of sin leads to a neutered Lamb and a neutered Lion. *And all put together, they add up to neutered preaching and religious meaninglessness.***

Perhaps our real problem with fearing God is that too many Christians have neutered the biblical concept of sin. We have forgotten the thunderous proclamations of Paul that "all have sinned and fall short of the glory of God" (Rom. 3:23) and that "the wages of sin is death" (Rom. 6:23). *A neutered understanding of sin leads to a neutered Lamb and a neutered Lion.* And all put together, *they add up to neutered preaching and religious meaninglessness.*

Revelation's Wake-up Call

The Apocalypse of John is a wake-up call to both the world at large and to Adventists in particular.

The Apocalypse of John is a summons to put away our casual attitude toward God and the issues of the great controversy and to address the real issues of the space/time world in which we live.

- For too long have we sought to make God into a nice twenty-first-century gentleman on the order of an Adventist intellectual or a kindly Loma Linda physician.
- For too long have we thought of God as a toothless old grandfather or as a figment of Uncle Arthur's bedtime stories in which all who are kind and good get eternal candy. C. S. Lewis caught the point when he suggested that what most people want is "not so much a Father in Heaven as a grandfather in heaven"—kind of a "senile benevolence."[15]

The Apocalypse of John is a judgment on all such thinking.

> *The call is to move beyond beastly preaching and other forms of neutering the apocalyptic vision and toward a renewed examination of the apocalyptic vision in relation to Adventism and the world for the twenty-first century.*

The Apocalypse of John is a judgment on the postmodern mentality that avoids any certainty in religious truth and seeks in its place a nebulous spirituality.

The Apocalypse of John is about a new heaven and a new earth.

The Apocalypse of John is about the Lamb and the Lion.

The Apocalypse of John is a call to Seventh-day Adventists to wake up not only to the beauty of the last book of the Bible, but to

(1) its power and forcefulness and

(2) its message for our day.

May God help us respond to the message of the book that made us a vibrant people. We have a message about the Lion and the Lamb that we are in danger of both distorting and losing.

The call is to move beyond beastly preaching and other forms of neutering the apocalyptic vision and toward a renewed examination of the apocalyptic vision in relation to Adventism and the world for the twenty-first century.

[1] Published with the same title in *Journal of Adventist Education,* April/May 2008, pp. 20-28.

[2] George R. Knight, *A Search for Identity: The Development of Seventh-day Adventist Beliefs* (Hagerstown, Md.: Review and Herald, 2000).

[3] Kenneth L. Woodward, "Dead End for the Mainline? Religion: The Mightiest Protestants Are Running Out of Money, Members, and Meaning," *Newsweek,* Aug. 9, 1993, pp. 46-48.

[4] *Ibid.,* pp. 48, 47.

[5] Thomas C. Reeves, *The Empty Church: The Suicide of Liberal Christianity* (New York: Free Press, 1996).

[6] Wade Clark Roof and William McKinney, *American Mainline Religion: Its Changing Shape and Future* (New Brunswick, N.J.: Rutgers University Press, 1987), pp. 234, 241.

[7] Roger Finke and Rodney Stark, *The Churching of America 1776-1990: Winners and Losers in Our Religious Economy* (New Brunswick, N.J.: Rutgers University Press, 1992), p. 238 (italics supplied.)

[8] Dean M. Kelley, *Why Conservative Churches Are Growing: A Study in Sociology of Religion* (New York: Harper and Row, 1972).

[9] Ellen G. White, *Gospel Workers* (Washington, D.C.: Review and Herald, 1948), p. 315.

[10] Ian Boxall, *The Revelation of Saint John,* Black's New Testament Commentaries (Peabody, Mass: Hendrickson, 2006), p. 33.

[11] See George R. Knight, *The Cross of Christ: God's Work for Us* (Hagerstown, Md.: Review and Herald, 2008).

[12] George Eldon Ladd, *A Commentary on the Revelation of John* (Grand Rapids: Eerdmans, 1972), p. 91.

[13] Ellen G. White, *The Desire of Ages* (Mountain View, Calif.: Pacific Press, 1940), p. 35.

[14] W. L. Walker, *What About the New Theology?* (Edinburgh: T. & T. Clark, 1907), pp. 48, 149.

[15] Alan Richardson, *An Introduction to the Theology of the New Testament* (New York: Harper and Row, 1958), p. 77.

[16] C. S. Lewis, *The Problem of Pain* (New York: Macmillan, 1962), p. 40.

Chapter 2

Another Look at Apocalyptic Prophecy and Adventist History

The first chapter introduced Christ as the slain Lamb and the Lion of the tribe of Judah, noting that if we have only the Lamb we possess only half a gospel. And, of course, if we have only the beasts we have no gospel at all. We need the Lord of the beasts. Revelation centers on Jesus as Lord of all.

This chapter will take a look at the apocalyptic vision and Adventist history. The topic is of the utmost importance because from its very beginning Seventh-day Adventism has viewed itself as a called out people with a prophetic mission. Adventism has never seen itself as just another denomination. It is that understanding that has given the Advent movement power. While the denomination is evangelical, it has never been merely evangelical. Rather, it has been evangelical with a prophetic message for the world centered on the Lamb of God and the apocalyptic Lion of the tribe of Judah.

The Prophetic Setting

An understanding of the apocalyptic vision and Adventist history begins in Revelation 10, which comes between the sixth (Rev. 9:13) and seventh (Rev. 11:15) trumpets. The identity of the trumpets is not always easy to unpack, but it is clear that the seventh trumpet is sounded at the Second Advent when "the kingdom of the world has become the kingdom of our Lord and of his Christ, and he shall reign for ever and ever" (Rev. 11:15).

Between the sixth and seventh trumpets we find Revelation 10 as an intermission or diversion from the flow of the trumpets. The central feature of the chapter is a little book or scroll opened in the hand of a "mighty angel" who had come down from heaven (verses 1, 2). The Greek tense signifies that it had once been shut but now has been opened. Thus right before the end of time the little scroll would be unrolled.

We find the little book again in verses 8-10: "Then the voice which I had heard from heaven spoke to me again, saying, 'Go, take the scroll which is open in the hand of the angel who is standing on the sea and on the land.' So I went to the angel and told him to give me the little scroll; and he said to me, 'Take it and eat; it will be bitter to your stomach, but sweet as honey in your mouth.' And I took the little scroll from the hand of the angel and ate it; it was sweet as honey in my mouth, but when I had eaten it my stomach was made bitter."

From its very beginning Seventh-day Adventism has viewed itself as a called out people with a prophetic mission. Adventism has never seen itself as just another denomination. It is that understanding that has given the Advent movement power. While the denomination is evangelical, it has never been merely evangelical.

Here we have a little book sealed up until the end of time. It is not the book or scroll of chapter 5, which is a big book identified by a different Greek word. The little book of Revelation 10 is related to the larger book that portrays the great events of eschatological history, but it has its own identity.

As the Millerites studied Revelation 10 they were forced to ask what little book had been sealed until the end of time. That question took them to Daniel 12:4: "But you, Daniel, shut up the words, and seal the book [or scroll], until the time of the end. Many shall run to and fro, and knowledge shall increase."

- In Revelation 10 we have a little book that is opened at the end of time.
- In Daniel 12 we have a book that is sealed until the end of time. And when it is opened knowledge shall increase.

We Adventists have done some strange things with Daniel 12:4. I have heard sermons explaining that for thousands of years people could move no faster than they could walk or ride a horse. But then we got steam power, automobiles, jet planes, and so on. And, as to knowledge, the store of it is growing so rapidly that it now doubles in ever shortening periods of time. Preachers and evangelists used such approaches to prove that we were in the time of the end and that Jesus would come soon.

But such presentations have nothing to do with the prophecy of Daniel 12:4. Rather, it is telling us that at the time of the end the eyes of men and women would run back and forth through the book of Daniel and knowledge of the book itself would increase as that book was unsealed.

One very interesting fact about the sealing of the book of Daniel is that the prophet only mentions two parts of his vision that were sealed. He is quite specific on that point. We will talk about both of them in chapter 3, but only one of them now.

In Revelation 10, we have a little book that is opened at the end of time. In Daniel 12 we have a book that is sealed until the end of time.

That takes us to Daniel 8, in which we find four great prophetic symbols—the ram of verse 3, the he-goat of verse 5, the little horn of verse 9, and the vision of the 2300 evenings and mornings, after which the sanctuary will be cleansed, justified, or restored to its rightful state (verse 14).

How do we know that we have only four prophetic symbols in chapter 8? Because Daniel calls for an explanation, and God sends the angel Gabriel. "When I, Daniel, had seen the vision, I sought to understand it; and behold, there stood before me one having the appearance of a man. And I heard a man's voice between the banks of the Ulai, and it called, 'Gabriel, make this man understand the vision'"—the vision of the first 14 verses. "So he came near where I stood; and when he came, I was frightened and fell on my face. But he said to me, 'Understand, O son of man, that *the vision is for the time of the end*'" (Dan. 8:15-17).

And then Gabriel launches into the explanation of the four symbols.

1. Verse 20: the ram is Media-Persia—hardly the time of the end.
2. Verse 21: the he-goat is Greece.
3. Gabriel's explanation of the little horn in verses 22-25 doesn't directly tell us what it is. Rather, it provides two identifying marks: in verse 24 that it would destroy the holy people and in verse 25 that it would "rise up against the Prince of princes." Thus the little horn power would not only destroy the Jewish nation but would stand up against God's Christ, the "King of kings and Lord of lords" (Rev. 19:16). Although not explicitly named, the identity of the third symbol is implicitly Rome.
4. And then the fourth symbol in verse 26: "The vision of the evenings and the mornings which has been told is true; but *seal up the vision, for it pertains to many days hence.*"

Only two things in Daniel are sealed until the time of the end and would be opened then. Daniel is very specific. One of them is the 2300-day prophecy. It would be sealed until the time of the end, and then the eyes of men and women would run to and fro through the book of Daniel and the 2300-day prophecy would be unsealed.

That thought takes us to world history, particularly to the French Revolution. The violence, its anti-Christian aspects, its total overthrow of accepted morality, and its various extremes led Christians around the world to claim that the event reminded them of the Bible's remarks about the trouble in the last days.

That understanding literally drove people to the prophecies of Daniel and Revelation. The next 50 years would see an outpouring of books on apocalyptic prophecy second to none in the history of Christianity. Truly the eyes of men and women were running to and fro through the book of Daniel and knowledge of his prophecies was increasing.[1]

Two prophecies particularly interested those searchers. One was the 1260 days, one of the two items in his book that Daniel tells us

> *Only two things in Daniel are sealed until the time of the end and would be opened then. Daniel is very specific. One of them is the 2300-day prophecy.*

were sealed (Dan. 12:9). We will return to the 1260 days in chapter 3. Meanwhile, this chapter will deal with the history of the Adventist understanding of apocalyptic prophecy, while the next will treat the exegetical basis of that history. Said in another way, it is one thing for our forebears to have arrived at prophetic conclusions, but it is quite another thing as to whether those conclusions have meaning for our day.

William Miller and the Rise of Adventism

In the years following the French Revolution Bible students on both sides of the Atlantic came to the conclusion that something had happened in the 1790s to fulfill the 1260-day prophecy and to initiate the time of the end of Daniel's prophecies.

One student of those prophecies is especially significant to Adventist history. William Miller had become a skeptical deist in early adulthood. Although Miller was certainly a talented individual, in his early years He hardly appeared to be a likely candidate for the ministry. He had, for example, much fun mimicking the holy sounds and intonations of his preacher grandfather, to the great delight of his beer hall audience.[2]

But his complacency came to an end during the United States' second war with Britain, which began in 1812. Serving as an army captain, Miller's experiences led him to the frightful conclusion that his deism had no answer to the problem of death, which had become very real to him as he witnessed comrades shot down.

By 1818 Miller had decided that Jesus would return in about 25 years. It compelled him to proclaim, "I need not speak of the joy that filled my heart." He had indeed found something that was "sweet in the mouth," and he looked longingly forward to a time that suffering and death would forever cease.

It drove him to the Bible to find meaning in a chaotic and destructive world. Miller went to God's Word, as did a whole generation of Europeans and European colonists in reaction to the excesses in France. In America the evangelical revival became known as the Second Great Awakening, during which many turned away from secular deism and toward Christianity. Miller was among that group.

Beginning to study his Bible in 1816, he soon was able to proclaim that "the Scriptures . . . became my delight, and in Jesus I found a friend."[3] A transformed man, Miller began to study the Bible intensely. From that point on, the study of the Bible from Genesis to Revelation dominated his life as his hours of daily study stretched through the years.

And he discovered things that he never expected to find. For example, as he studied the time prophecies of Daniel he came to the same conclusion as at least 80 published exegetes—that the fulfillment of the 2300-day prophecy that had been sealed up until the time of the end would take place sometime between 1843 and 1847.[4]

As Miller looked at the King James Version on the 2300-days ("unto two thousand and three hundred days; then shall the sanctuary be cleansed"), he was forced to ask himself what would happen at the end of that prophetic period. That led him to inquire as to the identity of the sanctuary and the cleansing of Daniel 8:14. After further study he concluded that the sanctuary that needed cleansing in the 1840s was the earth and that fire would be the cleansing agent. And when, he asked, will the earth be cleansed by fire? In the light of 2 Peter 3:11-13, he answered, When Jesus comes again![5]

Thus by 1818 Miller had decided that Jesus would return in about 25 years. It compelled him to proclaim, "I need not speak of the joy that filled my heart."[6] He had indeed found something that was "sweet in the mouth," and he looked longingly forward to a time that suffering and death would forever cease.

Unfortunately for him, Miller began to feel impressed that he should share his joyful discovery with others. But he feared that he might have made an error in his calculations. So he devoted another five years to the topic of the Second Advent and related issues. He especially wanted to examine every possible objection to his theory.

But at the end of five years he still didn't feel confident to speak publicly on the topic. So he spent another nine years on private study of the Bible. Yet by 1832 he still had no desire to open his mouth.

It appears that Miller was afflicted by *the sin of Bible study*, a widespread disease among church members. Now, Bible study is good in itself, but when you study it and study it and study it yet are not moved to action, then you can be sure that you have fallen into the pit of the sin of Bible study. Bible study without action is to miss the point. Bible study is to get us moving for God. Successful Bible study motivates us to get up from whatever we are sitting on and to tell people about Jesus—about what we have found.

Miller may have suffered from the sin of Bible study. But he couldn't escape his conscience, which kept urging him to "go and tell it to the world." His response was the Moses thing: "I'm not a good public speaker. I need a preacher to do it for me." But he couldn't find one. Although Miller tried every way he could think of to escape the conviction that he must say

> *Miller was afflicted by the sin of Bible study, a widespread disease among church members.*

something, he found no peace. "Go and tell it to the world" kept flashing through his mind.

Then one day in 1832, he later reported, "I sat down at my desk to examine some point; and as I arose to go out to work, it came home to me with more force than ever, 'Go and tell it to the world.' The impression was so sudden, and came with such force, that I settled down into my chair, saying, I can't go, Lord. 'Why not?' seemed to be the response; and then all my excuses came up, my want of ability, and etc.; but my distress became so great, I entered into a solemn covenant with God, that if he would open the way, I would go and perform my duty to the world. 'What do you mean by opening the way?' seemed to come to me. Why, said I, if I should have an invitation to speak publicly in any place, I will go and tell them what I find in the Bible about the Lord's coming."[7]

"Instantly," he tells us, "my burden was gone." He was more than happy with his agreement with God. After all, Miller was 50 years old, and never once had anyone asked him to preach in his entire life. At last he had peace with God and his nagging conscience.

But watch out what you promise God! Miller was in for a rude awakening. Within a half hour he had a boy at his door who had walked for 16 miles. The message was that his father needed Miller's help the next day. Being a justice of the peace, Miller assumed that the man wanted to see him on business.

But that comfortable supposition crashed to the floor when Miller inquired what the boy's father needed. "He replied that there was to be no preaching in their church the next day, and his father wished to have me come and talk to the people on the subject of the Lord's coming."

To put it mildly, Miller was angry with himself for having made the agreement with God. "I rebelled at once," he reported, and stomped out the door to a nearby grove of trees. "There," he recalls, "I struggled with the Lord for about an hour, endeavoring to release myself from the covenant I had made with him."[8]

But finding no relief, he returned to the house and told the visitor that he would do it. The next day's sermon brought converts. And thus began one of the most fruitful ministries in mid-nineteenth-century America. His message was the coming of the Lord "about the year 1843."

An interesting insight into Miller's understanding of the flow of prophecy appears in a time line he published in the *Signs of the Times* on May 1, 1841. In the period running from 1798 to 1843 Miller placed "Rev. Chap. 10. Opening of the Little Book. 45 Years to the End." He believed that the advent movement was a fulfillment of the prophecy dealing with the opening of the little scroll of Revelation 10 (see verses 8-10 and Daniel 12:4).[9]

With that fact in mind, I have a question I want to ask Miller when we get to heaven: "How come you didn't read all of Revelation 10:8-10?" After all, it not only said that the fulfillment of the prophecy would be sweet in the mouth, but also that it would be bitter in the belly. It is quite logical to conclude that if sweetness in the mouth reflected joy at the news of the Second Advent, then the bitterness would be tied to some sort of disappointment. From that perspective the chapter indicates that God knew about the disappointment before it ever happened. But apparently Miller wasn't any more perceptive than the 12 disciples to whom Christ repeatedly gave warnings of His forthcoming crucifixion. All any of them could see was the glory. Human beings seem to like sweetness more than bitterness.

William Miller read the book of Revelation like most of us. We grab hold of those things we think we understand and skip over those we don't. At any rate, Miller believed that the prophetic excitement that began in the 1790s had opened up the little book of Revelation 10.

It is quite logical to conclude that if sweetness in the mouth reflected joy at the news of the Second Advent, then the bitterness would be tied to some sort of disappointment. From that perspective the chapter indicates that God knew about the disappointment before it ever happened.

Now, Miller was smart enough not to assign any exact date to the Second Advent. After all, Jesus had plainly told His followers that no one knows the day or the hour (Matt. 24:36). So Miller would say only "about the year 1843." But by December 1842 his fellow believers were asking if he couldn't be more specific on the topic, since the year 1843 was just around the corner.

Miller believed that he could be more definite. After considering the typology of the Jewish religious year, he concluded that Christ would return between the Passover of 1843 and the Passover of 1844—that Jesus would come sometime between March 21, 1843, and March 21, 1844. That would be the year of the end of the world.

But March 21, 1844, arrived and went, and nothing happened. Millerism passed through its first, or spring, disappointment.

Then in the summer of 1844 a Methodist Millerite by the name of Samuel Snow announced to the believers that they had had it all wrong. Building upon a suggestion that Miller had published on May 17, 1843, Snow insisted that they shouldn't have been looking at Passover for the fulfillment of the 2300-day prophecy, but rather at the Day of Atonement. Miller had perceptively argued that, according to the New Testament,

Passover and all the first-month, or spring, feasts of the Jewish year had met their antitypical fulfillment at the first coming of Christ, whereas the autumn, or seventh-month, feasts would be fulfilled at the Second Advent. Snow, picking up Miller's logic, claimed that the sanctuary would be cleansed on the tenth day of the seventh Jewish month—on the Day of Atonement.[10] That day in 1844 would fall on October 22.

The new date didn't excite Miller. In fact, he didn't accept Snow's teaching until October 6, 1844. On that day he wrote for the Millerites' *Midnight Cry* a letter of sheer happiness on the topic. "I see a glory in the seventh month which I never saw before,"[11] he exclaimed.

We need to stop here and put ourselves in the place of Miller and the Adventists in October 1844. How excited we would be if we thought we could prove mathematically that Jesus would come in two weeks. That joyful expectation would dominate our lives as we shouted the message from the rooftops. There could be nothing sweeter or more fraught with excitement and joy. Jesus is coming in a few more days. To get the impact of the October 1844 movement we have to capture the historical moment from the inside as the Advent believers felt the joyful message in their very bones.

With that in mind, we will return to Miller's excited report to the believers on October 6, 1844. "I see a glory in the seventh month which I never saw before. Although the Lord had shown me the typical bearing of the seventh month, one year and a half ago [his May 17, 1843, article], yet I did not realize the force of the types. Now, blessed be the name of the Lord, I see a beauty, a harmony, and an agreement in the Scriptures, for which I have long prayed, but did not see until to-day.

"Thank the Lord, O my soul. Let Brother Snow, Brother Storrs and others, be blessed for their instrumentality in opening my eyes. I am almost home, Glory! Glory!! Glory!!! I see that the time is correct. . . .

"My soul is so full I cannot write. I call on you, and all who love his appearing, to thank him for this glorious truth. My doubts, and fears, and darkness, are all gone. I see that we are yet right. God's word is True; and *my soul is full of joy; my heart is full of gratitude to God.* Oh, how I wish I could shout. But I will shout when the 'King of kings comes.'

"Methinks I hear you say, 'Bro. Miller is now a fanatic.' Very well, call me what you please; I care not; Christ will come in the seventh month, and will bless us all. *Oh! glorious hope. Then I shall see him, and be like him, and be with him forever. Yes, forever and ever.*"[12]

The opening up of the little book had truly been sweet in the mouth. Jesus was returning in two weeks.

But October 22 came—and went. And Jesus didn't come.

Don't let anybody tell you that October 22 was the Great Disappointment. October 22 was the great anticipation. It was when the sun came up the next day that the disappointment hit with a smashing blow. It had been sweet in the mouth, but oh, how bitter in the belly.

On October 24 Josiah Litch (one of the foremost Millerite leaders) wrote to Miller from Philadelphia, noting that "it is a cloudy and dark day here—the sheep are scattered—and the Lord has not come yet."[13]

It was bitter in the belly.

Hiram Edson recalled that "our fondest hopes and expectations were blasted, and such a spirit of weeping came over us as I never experienced before. It seemed that the loss of all earthly friends could have been no comparison. We wept, and wept."[14]

It was indeed bitter in the belly.

James White reported that "the disappointment at the passing of the time was a bitter one. True believers had given up all for Christ, and had shared his presence as never before. . . . The love of Jesus filled every soul, and beamed from every face, and with inexpressible desires they prayed, 'Come Lord Jesus, and come quickly.' But he did not come. . . . I . . . wept like a child."[15]

Don't let anybody tell you that October 22 was the Great Disappointment. October 22 was the great anticipation. It was when the sun came up the next day that the disappointment hit with a smashing blow.

It had truly been sweet in the mouth, but it had just as certainly been bitter in the belly.

The October disappointment, with its specificity regarding an exact time, shattered the Millerite movement. But it wasn't the end of Revelation 10. After the sweet but bitter experience of verses 8-10 comes verse 11: "And he said unto me, Thou must prophesy again before many peoples, and nations, and tongues, and kings" (KJV). *Out of the ruins of that bitter experience, prophecy tells us, another movement would arise, one that would go to the ends of the earth.*

At this juncture I should note that as I see it the significance of Daniel 8:14 is not so much for personal salvation as it is an anchor point in time for a final world mission that would take a special message to every nation, tribe, and tongue (Rev. 10:11; 14:6). We will have more to say on that in chapter 3.

Discovering a Prophetic Message That Must Go to All the Earth

Meanwhile, we need to get back to the ruins of Millerism. Out of the chaotic conditions of post-Disappointment Millerism would arise three distinct movements. The first in the spring of 1845 proclaimed that they had been correct about Daniel 8:14 in terms of both time and the expected event. Jesus had come in October 1844, but He hadn't returned physically in the clouds of heaven. Rather, He spiritually entered into believers' hearts. And with that conclusion they began to explain away the literalness of Scripture.

The significance of Daniel 8:14 is not so much for personal salvation as it is an anchor point in time for a final world mission that would take a special message to every nation, tribe, and tongue (Rev. 10:11; 14:6).

A wide variety of fanaticisms arose among these "spiritualizers." Some of them said that when the kingdom came people would become like little children. So they gave up knives and forks, ate with their hands, and crawled around town to prove that they were indeed in the kingdom. And then there were the no-work Adventists, who proclaimed that since they were in the seventh millennium it was a sin to work. Another faction held that if they were in the kingdom it was impossible to sin. So they took spiritual husbands and spiritual wives, with some very earthly results.[16]

Fanaticism had broken loose. And if William Miller and Joshua V. Himes detested and feared one thing above anything else, it was fanaticism. As a result, they reacted to the spiritualizer fanatics by taking an alternative position on the fulfillment of prophecy in October 1844, claiming that they had been wrong on the time but right on the event. That is, no prophecy had come to fruition at that time but Daniel 8:14 did signal the end of the world. Many of those taking that position continued to set new dates, but the more dates they set, the more discouraged they became. This group probably had 50,000 members in it in the summer of 1845. But after repeated interpretive failures it would eventually give up Miller's understanding of prophecy.

There was a third orientation in relation to an October 1844 fulfill-ment of prophecy, but it didn't have any members in it in 1845 and 1846. What we find are individuals with a commitment to Bible study in the light of their Millerite experience. This third orientation would eventually conclude that prophecy had indeed been fulfilled in October 1844, but that they had been wrong on the event to take place. That is, they had been correct on the time, but wrong regarding what would happen.

That conclusion led to several people questioning the nature of the sanctuary and the cleansing of Daniel 8:14. Soon after the Disappointment they asked themselves: "If we were right on the time, what happened?" One of those individuals was O.R.L. Crosier, who began publishing a se-ries of articles on the sanctuary in early 1845 indicating that according to the book of Hebrews a sanctuary exists in heaven and that the cleansing of that sanctuary is not by fire but by the blood of Jesus. By early 1846 Crosier had arrived at an understanding of the two-phase ministry of Christ, with the second phase beginning in the Most Holy Place of the heavenly sanc-tuary in October 1844.[17]

Crosier didn't stand alone in publishing findings on the cleansing of the heavenly sanctuary. By April 1845 G. W. Peavey was writing about the sec-ond-phase ministry of Christ in the Most Holy Place in relation to October 1844. And by August he had seen an interrelationship between Daniel 8:14; Hebrews 9:23, 24; and Leviticus 16 and concluded that the Most Holy Place of the heavenly sanctuary needed purification by Christ's blood on the anti-typical day of atonement.

With his new understanding of Daniel 8:14 and the Most Holy Place of the heavenly sanctuary, Revelation's portrayal of the opening of the second apartment of that sanctuary at the end of time was not lost on Bates.

And then there was Emily C. Clemons, who edited a periodical in mid-1845 entitled *Hope Within the Veil.*

Thus by 1845 we find a number of Adventists tying the opening of Christ's second-phase ministry in the Most Holy Place of the heavenly sanctuary to October 1844. An ex-sea captain by the name of Joseph Bates early on accepted that position. As a result, he was impressed when he read Revelation 11:19: "Then God's temple in heaven was opened, and the ark of his covenant was seen within his temple." With his new understanding of Daniel 8:14 and the Most Holy Place of the heavenly sanctuary, Revelation's portrayal of the opening of the second apartment of that sanctuary at the end of time was not lost on Bates.[18]

But his attention especially focused on the revealing of the ark of the covenant, leading him to ask why it should be disclosed at that time in history. What significance did the opening have? Of course, he knew what was in the ark. His questions led him to Revelation 12.

Chapter 12 is a historical overview of the church from the time of the Christ child up to the end of time, climaxing with the contents of the ark in verse 17: "Then the dragon was angry with the woman, and went off to make war on the rest of her offspring, on those who keep the commandments of God." Suddenly Bates saw that near the end of time, when the second apartment of the heavenly sanctuary was opened, God's commandments would become an issue, and He would have a commandment-keeping people. Thus Joseph began to preach the keeping of *all* God's commandments at the end of time as a prophetic fulfillment.

Now, an emphasis on commandment obedience wasn't all that unique in mid-nineteenth-century America. Most people honored nine of the Ten Commandments. But Bates began to teach that the seventh-day Sabbath should be observed.

> *Bates saw that near the end of time, when the second apartment of the heavenly sanctuary was opened, God's commandments would become an issue, and He would have a commandment-keeping people. Thus Joseph began to preach the keeping of all God's commandments at the end of time as a prophetic fulfillment.*

And where, we must ask, did Bates get the Sabbath? From the Seventh Day Baptists. The Seventh Day Baptists have never been an evangelistic people. For example, in 1840 they had a membership of approximately 6,000 members in North America. By 2000 they had "grown" to 4,800. That is, over a 160-year period they had shrunk 20 percent. They had the truth about the Sabbath, but it never led to growth in their ranks.

But there was one time in their history that they did get evangelistic. Their General Conference records for 1841 and 1843 reflect discussions on the need to share their Sabbath understanding with other Christians. The next couple years saw concerted action to spread the Bible's teaching on the seventh-day Sabbath.

But no one was listening. No one, that is, except some Millerite Adventists. One of the more significant Seventh Day Baptists to interact with the Millerites was Rachel Oakes. By early 1844 she had not only accepted the Advent message, but also shared her Sabbath perspective with the Adventist congregation in Washington, New Hampshire. Several of the members of that congregation began observing the seventh-day Sabbath by spring 1844. The Washington congregation apparently influenced Thomas M. Preble, a Millerite pastoring a nearby Freewill Baptist church. Preble began observing the Sabbath in August 1844.

The Sabbath had become such an issue in Adventist circles by September 1844 that their leading periodical ran two extensive articles on the "problem." Their solution was simple enough. Let's keep quiet on this topic. We will be in heaven next month, and God will then settle the identity of the Sabbath.

The Sabbath had become such an issue in Adventist circles by September 1844 that their leading periodical ran two extensive articles on the "problem."

But they didn't get to heaven. And on February 28, 1845, Preble published a forceful article on the Sabbath in the *Hope of Israel*. A 12-page pamphlet entitled *A Tract, Showing That the Seventh Day Should Be Observed as the Sabbath, Instead of the First Day; "According to the Commandment"* soon followed.

Bates read Preble's material in early 1845 and traveled to Washington, New Hampshire, where he met with some of the Sabbathkeepers. He returned home on fire. That's when he encountered James Madison Monroe Hall on the bridge connecting Fairview and New Bedford, Massachusetts. Hall made the big mistake of asking Bates what was new.

Here it is helpful to know more about Bates' enthusiasm on the topic of the Sabbath. S. N. Haskell tells us that Joseph spent 10 days at his home in the early 1850s. Not only did he preach every evening on the Sabbath, but he conducted a running Bible study on the topic in the Haskell home that went from waking up in the morning to retiring in the evening, with intermissions only for meals and Bates' evening sermon. At the end of 10 days Haskell was a seventh-day man.

Well, we don't know how long Joesph Bates kept James Madison Monroe Hall on that bridge, but we do know that when Hall finally got off of it he was a Sabbathkeeper. In gratitude he named his only son Joseph Bates Hall.

But Bates didn't always have such good success. In August 1846, for example, he met a young Christian Connexion preacher and his girlfriend and gave them one of his famous frontal-assault Bible studies on the Sabbath. But James White and Ellen Harmon both rejected it. Ellen would later write that all that Bates could talk about was the Sabbath, as if the other nine commandments didn't exist.[19]

Two other things happened in August 1846. James and Ellen got married. And Bates wrote a little book called *The Seventh Day Sabbath, a Perpetual Sign*. It is not especially surprising that the first edition of the book presented a Seventh Day Baptist approach to the Sabbath rather than what would later become the Seventh-day Adventist understanding. The Baptists saw the Sabbath as the right day, but did not view it in terms of prophecy.

In the autumn of 1846 the newlyweds read *The Seventh Day Sabbath* and converted to Bates' view. Then late in the year Bates traveled to western New York to meet with Crosier and the other developers of the sanctuary theology.

Apparently his discussions in New York and with the Whites helped Bates to grasp the fuller significance of the Sabbath in its prophetic context in the book of Revelation. As a result, in January 1847 he published a new edition of *The Seventh Day Sabbath, a Perpetual Sign*. It contained

The Baptists saw the Sabbath as the right day, but did not view it in terms of prophecy.

only 14 new pages,[20] but those pages show a revolution in his thinking on the significance of the Sabbath. He had moved from a Seventh Day Baptist theology of the Sabbath to a Seventh-day Adventist position.

His new understanding built upon Revelation 12:17. It included not only a recognition of the importance of the commandments at the end of time, but also an indication that there would be conflict over those commandments near the conclusion of earthly history. Significantly, the 1847 edition moved beyond Revelation 12:17 into a fuller discussion of chapters 13 and 14, which expound upon the last-day dragon power and the last-day woman or church of that verse. Thus from a study of the Bible Bates developed the great controversy theology. Most of us have probably thought that it came from Ellen White. Not so. Joseph Bates had the whole package put together by January 1847.

Particularly important for him was Revelation 14. In verse 6 he read: "Then I saw another angel flying in midheaven, with an eternal gospel to proclaim to those who dwell on earth, to every nation and tribe and tongue and people." And here we find an echo from Revelation 10:11, which tells us that after the sweet but bitter experience of the opening of the little book of Daniel there would be another message that must go to all the world. In chapter 14 we find that message.

From a study of the Bible Bates developed the great controversy theology. Most of us have probably thought that it came from Ellen White. Not so. Joseph Bates had the whole package put together by January 1847.

Bates began to put the pieces together. He moved on from Revelation 14:6 to verse 7, in which he read, "He said with a loud voice, 'Fear God and give him glory, for the hour of his judgment has come; and worship him who made heaven and earth, the sea and the fountains of water.'" The latter part of that verse especially caught Bates' eye. Here he saw a clear reference to the fourth commandment of Exodus 20:8-11, in which the rationale for the command to keep the seventh day is couched in the phrase "in six days the Lord made heaven and earth, the sea, and all that is in them" (verse 11; cf. Gen. 2:1-3). Thus Bates perceived that the issue at the end of time would not merely be the commandments of God (Rev. 12:17; 14:12), but especially the Sabbath commandment, which the first angel's message highlights.

More important yet in Revelation 14:7 is the issue of worship. Worship is a key word or concept in Revelation 13 and 14, appearing at least eight times. While verse 7 tells us that some will be worshipping the Creator God of the Sabbath of Genesis 2 and Exodus 20, verse 9 notes that others will be worshipping "the beast and its image." Everybody will be worshipping somebody at the end of time. Bates saw that clearly as he developed understandings on such topics as the seal of God and the mark of the beast.

Here we need to note again that the great controversy theology (that near the end of earth's history there will be war in heaven over God's commandments) is not some Seventh-day Adventist theological aberration that came through Ellen White. To the contrary, it is in the Bible, and we can't solve our problems on the topic by dumping her because she had a nineteenth-century perspective. No, one has to discard Scripture itself. By 1847 Bates had developed great controversy theology from the Bible without the benefit of Ellen White. Her first statement on the topic would come four months after he published his understanding when she had a vision confirming his great controversy perspective.[21]

Worship is a key word or concept in Revelation 13 and 14, appearing at least eight times. While Revelation 14:7 tells us that some will be worshipping the Creator God of the Sabbath of Genesis 2 and Exodus 20, verse 9 notes that others will be worshipping "the beast and its image." Everybody will be worshipping somebody at the end of time.

Along with Revelation 14:7 with its command to worship the Creator God Bates read the second angel's message in verse 8: "Fallen, fallen is Babylon the great," that is, those who have confused the Word of God with the words of people.

Next he went to verses 9-12, which in effect contrast the worshippers of the beast (verse 9) with those who have the patience of the saints and "keep the commandments of God and the faith of Jesus" (verse 12).

Following the third angel's message of verses 9-12, verse 13 provides readers with a flashback to chapter 13 with its description of the last-day conflict between those who submit to the beast power and those who worship God. Finally, verses 14-20 tell of Christ coming in the clouds of heaven to harvest the earth.

By January 1847 Bates clearly recognized that God would have a last-day people who would preach the three angels' messages right before the Second Advent. He had concluded that the evolving Sabbatarian Adventist orientation was a movement of prophecy.

Thus by 1848 the people who were becoming Sabbatarian Adventists had a message that excited them and gave direction to their evangelism, and they began to gather in a people. The results were exciting. Between late 1848 and early 1853 the movement zipped from about 100 members to some 2,500. Talk about church growth. They had a message, and they knew it.

For the next several decades they would preach their message with vigor. But please remember that they lived in a largely Christian culture. In such a world they saw little need to present grace to Baptists or prayer to Methodists. Such groups already had those things. What did they need? Those teachings, the logic ran, that they didn't have, such as the Sabbath, the state of the dead, and the sanctuary.

As a result, Adventist evangelism centered on doctrinal areas in which they differed from other Christians. Adventist evangelists would go into a community and challenge the foremost preacher to a debate (or public argument) on which day is the Sabbath or what happens when a person dies. And in a world short in entertainment it wasn't difficult to draw a crowd with such tactics. After all, the best show in town was two preachers getting into an argument.

But 40 years of such preaching led to two results. First, we often won the battles because the Bible was on our side. But, second, it brought in a lot of argumentative Adventists. And by the 1880s we discovered not only that we had become experts at arguing with other people, but that we could argue among ourselves.

> *By January 1847 Bates clearly recognized that God would have a last-day people who would preach the three angels' messages right before the Second Advent. He had concluded that the evolving Sabbatarian Adventist orientation was a movement of prophecy.*

Making Adventism Christian

Forty years of preaching on where we differ from others (definitely a form of beastly preaching) led to a disjunction between Adventism and basic Christianity. It was time for a reformation. That reformation would begin to take place at the 1888 General Conference session at Minneapolis, Minnesota. It centered on one text: "Here is the patience of the saints: here are they that keep the commandments of God, and the faith of Jesus" (Rev. 14:12, KJV).

The two sides in the 1888 struggle zeroed in on different aspects of that central text in Adventist history. The General Conference leadership,

G. I. Butler and Uriah Smith, focused on the part about keeping the commandments. To them that was the issue of issues in Adventism.

And in that position they were in longstanding company. James White had established the traditional Adventist understanding of Revelation 14:12 in 1850, when he saw three parts to the text. God's last-day people would be

(1) patiently waiting for Jesus to come;
(2) keeping all of God's commandments;
(3) keeping the faith of Jesus, which to White included such things as baptism and the Lord's Supper.[22]

Forty years of preaching on where we differ from others (definitely a form of beastly preaching) led to a disjunction between Adventism and basic Christianity. It was time for a reformation. That reformation would begin to take place at the 1888 General Conference session.

That was the primary interpretation of Revelation 14:12 up until 1888. In both of the last parts of the text the early Adventists found things to do. Thus J. N. Andrews could emphasize that "the faith" or the "faith of Jesus . . . is spoken of as being kept in the same manner that the commandments of God are kept." To him it was important to keep or obey both the commandments of God and the commands of Jesus.[23] In like manner, R. F. Cottrell wrote that the faith of Jesus "is something to be obeyed or kept. Therefore we conclude that all that we are required to do in order to be saved from sin belongs to the faith of Jesus."[24] Needless to say, Adventism in following that logic Adventism had become very legalistic. Going clear back to Joseph Bates, there had been a strong current that people are saved by keeping the commandments.

It was in that context that two young men who had a different understanding of Revelation 14:12 arose. A. T. Jones and E. J. Waggoner held that the last part of the verse meant "faith *in* Jesus," which is a valid translation of the Greek.

The one clearest on the new perspective would be Ellen White. The message given at Minneapolis, she asserted, was "not alone the commandments of God—a part of the third angel's message—but the faith of Jesus, which comprehends more than is generally supposed." The third angel's message needs "to be proclaimed in all its parts. . . . If we proclaim the commandments of God and leave the other half scarcely touched the message is marred in our hands."[25]

Soon after the Minneapolis meetings Ellen White made one of her most powerful statements on Revelation 14:12. "The third angel's message," she penned, "is the proclamation of the commandments of God and the faith of Jesus Christ. The commandments of God have been pro-

It was its prophetic understanding that empowered Seventh-day Adventism and made it a dynamic force.

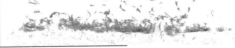

claimed, but the faith of Jesus Christ has not been proclaimed by Seventh-day Adventists as of equal importance, the law and the gospel going hand in hand." She went on to discuss the meaning of the faith of Jesus, which "is talked of, but not understood." The faith of Jesus, she claimed, means "Jesus becoming our sin-bearer that He might become our sin-pardoning Saviour. . . . He came to our world and took our sins that we might take His righteousness. Faith in the ability of Christ to save us amply and fully and entirely is the faith of Jesus."[26]

Adventism got rebaptized at Minneapolis in 1888 as church members began to see Jesus and faith in Him as its center. Along that line, Ellen White told the 1888 General Conference delegates that "we want the truth as it is in Jesus. . . . I have seen that precious souls who would have embraced the truth have been turned away from it because of the manner in which the truth has been handled, because Jesus was not in it. And this is what I have been pleading with you for all the time—we want Jesus."[27] Again, "My burden during the meeting was to present Jesus and His love before my brethren, for I saw marked evidences that many had not the spirit of Christ."[28]

Beginning in 1888 Adventism had recovered a balanced message. As a result, Ellen White could claim that we finally had the loud cry message.[29] Here was a people who were waiting for Jesus to come. And while patiently waiting, they were keeping God's commandments from their hearts and maintaining a saving faith in Jesus.

In conclusion, I need to reiterate that the founders of Adventism found the significance of their movement in the prophetic package of Revelation 14 with its progressive flow from the first angel's message to the second angel's message to the third angel's message and on to the eschaton. They saw themselves as a called-out people with a special end-time message to present to all the world. It was that prophetic understanding that empowered Seventh-day Adventism and made it a dynamic force.

Getting Priorities Straight

But having said that, I also need to emphasize that having a sense of prophetic calling is not all there is to being a people whom God can bless. Some Adventists have gone off the track here, confusing the outward teachings and practices of Christianity with the real thing. There is, for example, a huge difference between keeping Saturday and observing the Sabbath. People can keep Saturday because it's the right day, yet be totally lost. But they can observe Sabbath only with Jesus in their hearts. The emphasis on worship in Revelation 14:7 suggests that the issue is much more than which day one outwardly honors. It has to do with whether one has a saving relationship with the Creator God. What we need is a transforming heart relationship and not merely correct doctrines and good lifestyle practices.

God wants a people who love Him and serve Him from their hearts.

> *The emphasis on worship in Revelation 14:7 suggests that the issue is much more than which day one outwardly honors. It has to do with whether one has a saving relationship with the Creator God.*

Some years ago I was preaching in Ohio on my favorite text—John 13:35: "By this all men will know that you are my disciples, because you keep the Sabbath." I love that text.

After my sermon a new convert approached me and said, "Brother Knight, I can't find that text in my Bible." He was undoubtedly looking for the perfect proof text to take home to his family.

"Brother," I said, "you weren't listening very carefully." And then I repeated the actual wording of John 13:35: "By this all men will know that you are my disciples, if you have love for one another." That's where the action is. Dynamic Christianity is becoming more and more like the God who is love (1 John 4:8). We are truly keeping God's commandments only when our actions flow out of a heartfelt love for Him and other people. Without that love we are only imitating that commandment keeping that is related to the faith of Jesus. The absence of that all-important motivational force is why some people keep the right day and eat the right things but are meaner than the devil.

Some of us Adventists think we have "the truth." But when I go to certain of our churches I wonder. I once went to an Adventist church, and no one said hello to me. Now, I didn't want to make them feel uncomfortable, so I never said anything either. I just sat down. There was only one thing they didn't know—that I was the speaker for the day.

About 11:05 you could feel that something was wrong. Finally somebody tapped me on the shoulder, asking me if I was the speaker. Good guess, but not all that difficult since I was the only visitor.

And so I got up to preach. And halfway through my sermon I stopped, paused, and finally asked, "If you weren't an Adventist and you visited this church, would you ever come a second time?" Then I told them the truth: "I wouldn't, and I'm an Adventist."

The whole point is that if all that we have is the commandments of God and the patience of the saints, we don't have anything. We are not partially lost—we are totally lost.

God wants us to have the faith of Jesus. And when we know that we are saved by grace, we can't be proud and unloving. Reflecting on Ephesians 2:8, 9 ("For by grace you have been saved through faith; . . . not because of works, lest any man should boast"), D. L. Moody once noted that "if anybody ever gets to heaven by anything they ever did, we'll never hear the end of it." Being saved by grace both humbles and softens us.

> *God wants us to be well balanced in our apocalyptic message. The truth with a small "t"—doctrinal truth—is important, but only so if it is embedded in the truth with a capital "T"—Jesus Christ crucified, resurrected, coming again in the clouds of heaven.*

I believe that God has a message for our day. I believe that we need to preach Jesus coming in the clouds of heaven. I believe that we ought to teach the Ten Commandments and the Sabbath. But if we stop there, we are only Adventists. We have to move on to the faith of Jesus.

God has a message. By 1888 some Adventists had put the picture together: Here is a people patiently waiting for Jesus to come, and while waiting they are keeping the commandments of God and have saving faith in Jesus. Such Adventism is contexted in a vibrant relationship with Jesus as Lord and Savior.

And God wants us to be well balanced in our apocalyptic message. The truth with a small "t"—doctrinal truth—is important, but only so if it is embedded in the truth with a capital "T"—Jesus Christ crucified, resurrected, coming again in the clouds of heaven.

---

[1] See LeRoy Edwin Froom, *The Prophetic Faith of Our Fathers: The Historical Development of Prophetic Interpretation* (Hagerstown, Md.: Review and Herald, 1982), vol. 3, pp. 270, 271.

[2] For a fuller treatment of William Miller and the rise of Adventism, see George R. Knight, *Millennial Fever and the End of the World: A Study of Millerite Adventism* (Boise, Idaho: Pacific Press, 1993).

[3] William Miller, *Wm. Miller's Apology and Defence* (Boston: J. V. Himes, 1845), pp. 4, 5.

[4] Froom, vol. 4, p. 404.

[5] William Miller, *Letter to Joshua V. Himes, on the Cleansing of the Sanctuary* (Boston: Joshua V. Himes, 1842).

[6] Miller, *Apology and Defence*, p. 12.

[7] *Ibid.*, pp. 15-17.

[8] *Ibid.*, p. 18.

[9] William Miller, "Chronological Chart of the World," *Signs of the Times*, May 1, 1841, p. 20.

[10] Samuel S. Snow, in *The True Midnight Cry*, Aug. 22, 1844; William Miller, "Letter From Wm. Miller," *Signs of the Times,* May 17, 1843, p. 85.

[11] William Miller, "Brother Miller's Letter, on the Seventh Month," *The Midnight Cry,* Oct. 12, 1844, p. 121.

[12] *Ibid.* (Italics supplied.)

[13] Josiah Litch to William Miller and Joshua V. Himes, Oct. 24, 1844.

[14] Hiram Edson, unpublished manuscript fragment. This document and many others in the notes for this chapter have been published in George R. Knight, comp. and ed., *1844 and the Rise of Sabbatarian Adventism* (Hagerstown, Md.: Review and Herald, 1994).

[15] James White, *Life Incidents* (Battle Creek, Mich.: Seventh-day Adventist Pub. Assn., 1868), p. 182.

[16] On the rise of the various post-Disappointment movements, see Knight, *Millennial Fever*, pp. 245-325.

[17] For the most complete account of the rise of Sabbatarian Adventist theology, see Merlin D. Burt, "The Historical Background, Interconnected Development, and Integration of the Doctrines of the Sanctuary, the Sabbath, and Ellen G. White's role in Sabbatarian Adventism From 1844 to 1849" (Ph.D. dissertation, Andrews University, 2002). For an abbreviated published version, see Knight, *A Search for Identity*, pp. 55-89.

[18] For more on the massive contribution of Joseph Bates to the development of Seventh-day Adventist theology, see George R. Knight, *Joseph Bates: The Real Founder of Seventh-day Adventism* (Hagerstown, Md.: Review and Herald, 2004), pp. 107-151.

[19] Ellen G. White, *Spiritual Gifts* (Battle Creek, Mich.: James White, 1860), vol. 2, p. 82.

[20] Joseph Bates, *The Seventh-day Sabbath, a Perpetual Sign*, 2nd. ed. (New Bedford, Mass.: Benjamin Lindsey, 1847). See pp. iii, iv, 49-60 for the crucial additions to the 1846 treatment.

[21] Ellen G. White to Joseph Bates, Apr. 7, 1847. In James White, ed., *A Word to the "Little Flock"* (n.p.: James White, 1847), pp. 18-20.

[22] James White, "The Third Angel's Message," *Present Truth*, April 1850, pp. 66, 67.

[23] John N. Andrews, *The Three Messages of Revelation XIV, 6-12,* 5th ed. (Battle Creek, Mich.: Review and Herald, 1886), pp. 135, 129.

[24] R. F. Cottrell, *The Bible Class: Lessons Upon the Law of God, and the Faith of Jesus* (Rochester, N.Y.: Advent Review, 1855), pp. 62, 124.

[25] Ellen G. White, "Experiences Following the 1888 Minneapolis Conference," manuscript 30, 1889 (late June 1889). For an overview of the theological implications of the 1888 General Conference session, see George R. Knight, *A User-friendly Guide to the 1888 Message* (Hagerstown, Md.: Review and Herald, 1998).

[26] Ellen G. White, "Looking Back at Minneapolis," manuscript 24, 1888 (Nov. 1888).

[27] *Ibid.*

[28] Ellen G. White, "Morning Talk," manuscript 9, Oct. 24, 1888.

[29] Ellen G. White, "The Perils and Privileges of the Last Days," *Review and Herald*, Nov. 22, 1892, p. 722.

Chapter 3

But Don't Forget the Beasts
(Including the Modern Ones)
and My Problem With Apocalyptic

I once met a student of the Bible who on the basis of his esoteric and extensive knowledge of Greek, Hebrew, Aramaic, Ugaritic, Urdu, and Egyptian hieroglyphics all factored through the systematic theology of Paul Tillich and the existential philosophy of Jean-Paul Sartre and enriched by postmodern insights could prove beyond the shadow of a doubt that (1) nothing means nothing and that (2) smart, sophisticated people have no solid convictions except as they relate to subjectivity and uncertainty.

All of which proved to me what I already feared—that I was neither smart nor sophisticated.

The Importance of the Big Picture

Because of my unsophisticated nature I find a great deal of theological discussion to be entertaining but not necessarily meaningful. Let me illustrate. As I see it, most theological battles take place among the twigs and the leaves of the theological tree, with one person advocating one position on twig x and the other some variant theory. The mental gymnastics often leave me somewhat mystified if not unbalanced and dizzy.

In order to get some relief, I have developed the self-defensive but rather commonsense measure of checking to see if the tree has a trunk and if the leaves and twigs are connected to the trunk in any meaningful way. That little exercise puts things in perspective and frees me from a lot of interesting but not especially pertinent theological argumentation.

Said a bit differently, I am a big-picture sort of person. My approach is to look at the trunk and the general shape of the theological tree. And to put it in a more homely way yet, I pride myself in the fact that I can identify a tree when I see one.

This chapter will take a look at the big picture of the apocalyptic prophecies of Daniel and Revelation that have made Adventism a vibrant movement. The first chapter focused on the fact that the book of Revelation centers on Christ as the slain Lamb and the victorious Lion of the tribe of Judah. Put the two symbols together and you have the core of the gospel— that Christ died for our sins, resurrected and has the keys to the grave, and will eventually return to put an end to sin and suffering. Take away any aspect of that picture and you have neutered the Christian/Adventist message. As we noted, the Lamb without the Lion is a partial gospel.

The second chapter examined the rise of Adventism as it related to the apocalyptic vision. We discovered that the Seventh-day Adventist pioneers had seen the big picture and put together a theological package whose logical force has driven Adventism to every corner of the earth.

In this third chapter we want in part to stand back with both eyes open to see if early Adventism's apocalyptic understanding has validity and relevance for the twenty-first century. I must admit that I was daunted by the challenge of this chapter and how to say what needs to be said in such a short space. After all, during the past 30 years we have seen a dismantling of the apocalyptic vision by Adventist thinkers on one side and defensive reactions on the other. And then we witness a never-ending parade of apocalyptic cranks whose special burden is to prove something unique or at least strange from the words of Revelation. I felt challenged to say the least.

My first meeting with a certain Adventist intellectual didn't help my insecurities any. After talking over Adventism a bit, he wondered out loud how someone as smart as I was could believe all that stuff. I responded with the suggestion that I didn't see why someone as intelligent as he was would remain in Adventism if he didn't believe it.

And I still hold that conviction. To put it as frankly as possible, if Adventism's apocalyptic big picture isn't valid, the most sensible thing is to shut up shop, go home, and do something meaningful with our lives. If Adventism's big picture lacks meaning, I would like to suggest that the title for the next generation of Ph.D.s in Adventist studies be "Curators of Adventist Antiquities for Those Who Still Have Some Reason to Care."

The greatest threat to Adventism today is that of losing its understanding of the big picture of apocalyptic, which has made it a unique and vital people. Early Adventists read Revelation 14:6 about proclaiming the everlasting gospel "to every nation and tribe and tongue and people" and concluded that God had called them to take the messages of the three angels of Revelation 14:6-12 to all the world in preparation for the Advent pictured immediately following those messages (verses 14-20).

An understanding of that apocalyptic vision literally drove church members to sacrifice their lives and their money to spread what they called "the message." As I noted earlier, my wife's family was inspired by "the message" and "the mission." Her great-grandfather had the unlikely name of James Bond. No, he wasn't the real one, but having fathered 12 children, he was equally heroic. And nearly all of them went into "the work," with at least one laying his bones in a strange land and others facing persecution for the Advent cause.

If Adventism's apocalyptic big picture isn't valid, the most sensible thing is to shut up shop, go home, and do something meaningful with our lives

Such dedication is not a casual enterprise. It takes conviction to motivate sacrificial action—a conviction that Adventism has a message that is not only true and important, but one the world needs to hear in preparation for the Second Advent.

In 1888 a reporter for the Minneapolis *Journal* caught the centrality of the impact of the "arrogance" of Adventism's self-understanding as he wrote that when they applied Revelation 14:12 to themselves it was either because of fanatical egotism or a sublime faith. I trust that it was a sublime faith, one that moved them to action and sacrifice. By the 1890s Adventism was a people on the move.

But, as I noted in chapter 1, developed Adventism in the world sectors in the early twenty-first century has been tamed if not neutered. We have done such a good job of telling people that we are like other evangelicals (except for Sabbath and a few additional things) that we have forgotten who we are, forgotten what makes us unique, forgotten what gives our existence meaning. Thus the shrinkage among born-in-America members in all four major population groups of the North American Division (the same dynamic holds in most other developed nations). And thus the aging of the membership. The average age in the North American Division is 58, and given the fact that the other ethnic sectors of the church tend to have younger members, it is undoubtedly higher than 58 for the division's White membership. And it is hard to avoid the fact that an aging church can become a dying church.

Have we nothing to inspire young adults? Have we nothing that not only leads them to remain in Adventism but to dedicate their lives to "the cause"? What does it take to inspire them?

- Not the fact that we are like everybody else, but that Adventism stands for something important, that Seventh-day Adventism makes a difference.
- Young people are idealistic by nature, even in the face of adults who have been jaded by time and trials.
- Young people are energized by visions that give life meaning. It was so among the founders of Adventism. It was so in my life when grasping the apocalyptic vision transformed my listlessness and hedonistic purposelessness into meaning and mission. And I find that it is still so among young people in our day.

But if I were the devil I would tempt Adventists and their preachers to be just nice evangelicals and forget about such nasty stuff as apocalyptic. And if that didn't work I would tempt them to beastly preaching that focused on the details and the esoteric and extremes. I would get them arguing over 666 and the identity of the 144,000. And if that didn't succeed, I would get them to focus on excitement and apocalyptic fearmongering. And of course I would sow doubts in their minds about the validity of Adventism's basic apocalyptic understandings.

We have done such a good job of telling people that we are like other evangelicals (except for Sabbath and a few additional things) that we have forgotten who we are, forgotten what makes us unique, forgotten what gives our existence meaning.

We have a pretty smart devil. He has driven Adventists and their preachers off a balanced view of apocalyptic in almost every direction. And in the process he has all too often gotten us to perform the neutering task on our own selves.

Remembering the Beasts

In chapter 1 I noted the centrality of Christ to the book of Revelation. The Lamblike Lion is the crucial element. At the same time I pointed out that Adventism has heard too much beastly preaching.

But just because we have suffered from beastly preaching does not mean that the beasts are unimportant or that we should avoid them. Why?

Because God's Word doesn't ignore the beasts. In fact, the apocalyptic books of Daniel and Revelation are big on beasts. And here we need some insight into their nature. The book of Daniel is helpful on the topic. For example, Nebuchadnezzar saw the picture of world empires from the perspective of rulership. To him they were like a beautiful and precious image. But when Daniel viewed the same empires in chapter 7 from the perspective of God's people, they were ferocious beasts that ripped, tore, and destroyed. Revelation reflects that same picture in chapters 13-18.

How can a nation run over by both Hitler and Stalin say that beasts are out of date? The beast powers of prophecy may have started with Babylon and Persia, but they didn't stop there.

Apocalyptic prophecy is big on beasts.

A second reason that we should not forget the beasts in our day is that beasts are relevant. But not everybody thinks so. Some years ago I was preaching on Adventism and the apocalyptic vision in a certain European nation. Halfway through my meetings I was notified that "the people" (i.e., certain leaders and some of the people) didn't want to hear about the apocalyptic vision—that beasts and all that "stuff" are out-of-date.

Really? How can a nation run over by both Hitler and Stalin say that beasts are out-of-date? The beast powers of prophecy may have started with Babylon and Persia, but they didn't stop there. No Kurd under the chemical guns of Saddam Hussein argued that beasts are irrelevant. We will be dealing with beasts until the end of world history. To put it bluntly, we live in a beastly world. *Beasts are relevant.*

Of course, not all the beasts of Bible prophecy are nasty creatures. Some are lamblike. Lamblike beasts exist in our day, even ones with the potential to speak like a dragon.

I vividly recall a series of meetings I was holding in Switzerland for university students from across Europe. It was the first week of the latest invasion of Iraq, and the students were agitated. What right, they asked, did the United States have to invade other nations whenever it decided to?

That wasn't a particularly comfortable question for an American university professor. My response was that the Bible presents two types of beastly (government) powers—nasty beasts and lamblike beasts. The latter do everything in the name of democracy, goodness, and righteousness. It just so happens that today the world has only one super power that no one can stand against—a good, lamblike, "Christian" beast. And who can stand against its heat-seeking smart bombs that can zero in on the remotest buried bunkers? I concluded my remarks by noting that I didn't know much about the full exegesis or implications of Revelation 13, but that I could see with my own eyes in the world around me more than one beastly type or pattern with implications for both the present and the future.

Beasts are relevant in the twenty-first century, and they will be until the end of time. Such beasts and their deeds are the stuff of daily headlines and television news. We live in a beastly world that will not be debeastified until the King of kings and Lord of lords arrives in the clouds of heaven.

Thus while it is important to avoid beastly preaching, it is crucial not to forget the beastly highlights of the great controversy that run from Nebuchadnezzar through Persia, Greece, and Rome up to our day.

Connected to the beasts is the larger prophetic package related to Adventism's distinctive beliefs, such as the eschatological implications of the Sabbath, the sanctuary, the state of the dead, and so on—all presented from the perspective of the redeeming Christ who is central to the apocalyptic vision of John. Thus "not forgetting the beasts" includes the preaching of all of Adventism's distinctive message in a Christ-centered apocalyptic context.

Too many Adventists in their desire to be like everybody else have concluded that it is not helpful to preach doctrine at church services. The result: growing ignorance among the membership about why

> *While it is important to avoid beastly preaching, it is crucial not to forget the beastly highlights of the great controversy that run from Nebuchadnezzar through Persia, Greece, and Rome up to our day.*

they are going to church. One pastor recently told me that his non-Adventist mother has been regularly attending the Adventist congregation near her home for six years but still doesn't have the foggiest notion about the state of the dead. A couple months ago I preached a sermon entitled "Why Be Adventist?" in my local church. The "converts" are still coming out of the nooks and crannies telling me that the message helped them make sense out of their lives. The plain fact is that many, including those raised in the church, really have no grasp of why they are Adventist or even if it makes any real difference. Encouraged by the response, I am beginning a series of Christ-centered messages in my local congregation, including "Good News About the Sabbath," "Good News From the Heavenly Sanctuary," "The Judgment Is Good News—Gospel," and so on.

In short, it's not a sin to preach either apocalyptic or doctrine on Sabbath. We need to remember that the truths that brought people into Adventism will refresh their vision and enliven their faith. But please remember that when we present those topics disconnected from Christ and God's love, the message is beastly.

Another way to beastify and thereby neuter the apocalyptic message is to claim too much. We need to avoid the temptation toward being overly specific and dogmatic about the details of prophecy or being overly triumphalistic. It is important to remember that the exact fulfillment of prophecy is best seen after the event and that every generation of Christians has been able to find hope and comfort in Revelation's prophetic symbols.

Of course, at the other extreme from claiming to know too much is taking the position that we know too little about the apocalyptic vision. That thought brings me to my personal struggles with apocalyptic.

My Problem With Apocalyptic

To tell you the truth, I don't know nearly as much as I would like to about the Revelation of John. I certainly don't "know" as much as I did as a freshman theology major in college back when I had all the answers. Since then I have discovered that the intellectual journey is like crawling through a funnel backward. The further I go, the worse it gets; the further I go, the more I realize how vast are the data banks of knowledge. And like many other Adventists, I arrived at theological maturity by having traveled through an era of doubts regarding the Adventist message on one hand and apocalyptic bashing on the other.

It is an interesting fact that Adventism today has the highest educated clergy and laity in its history. Yet all too many of us are afraid to affirm much of anything, unless it's our doubts. That's stylish. But to affirm Adventism's distinctive truths, and especially to do so in relation to apocalyptic prophecy, gets one labeled as an irrelevant nineteenth-century sort of person in many circles. "Let's get real" is the response.

Now, I recognize that some of our preachers and lay members have been wrong in their claims. And I acknowledge that some of us Adventists have been disgustingly arrogant in our interpretations and attitudes.

But the answer is not to throw out the baby with the bathwater and pretend that Daniel and Revelation don't exist as prophetic documents or that they are concerned primarily with worship or social justice. The apocalyptic vision of John is concerned with both of those topics, but its primary function is to introduce us to the glorious Jesus who will put an end to all misery and injustice through the mode of the Second Advent.

In this chapter I want to list those aspects of apocalyptic that have troubled me. Beyond that, I want to expose my own conclusions and convictions. Needless to say, I will focus on the big picture in both apocalyptic prophecy and Adventist theology.

Before beginning, I should point out that Adventism has only one real theological problem—Jesus hasn't returned. But that problem brings every other in its train. Frustration regarding it has led to apocalyptic spin-offs in nearly every direction.

Historicism

In our survey of apocalyptic issues I will seek to deal with the big items. For starters, I tried to doubt the historicist prophetic framework, which asserts that apocalyptic prophecy begins at the time of the prophet and has more or less continuous fulfillment until the eschaton. And why shouldn't I doubt that position? After all, few non-Adventist biblical scholars are historicists in our day. As European scholar Kai Arasola's Ph.D. research demonstrates, the Millerite crisis of the 1840s spelt the end of historicism as a major interpretive school.[1] Most students of apocalyptic today are preterists (who hold that prophecy

Adventism has only one real theological problem—Jesus hasn't returned. But that problem brings every other in its train.

was for the time of the prophet), or futurists (who regard the main focus of apocalyptic prophecy as being on the short period right before Jesus returns), or those who see prophecy as being unrelated to time. In the face of the continuing delay of the Second Coming some Adventist interpreters of Revelation have stepped off of the historicist platform and onto that of futurism or preterism. Continuing time has had a corrosive effect on Adventist thinking. I can understand that.

But my doubting of historicism got hung up on the remarkable prophecy of Daniel 2, which presents four kingdoms ruling the biblical world from the time of Babylon to the fall of Rome and then a divided world in which no one can put the pieces back together until the end of time, when God sets up "a kingdom which shall never be destroyed" but will "break in pieces" the kingdoms of this world (Dan. 2:44).

It is all too easy to downplay the power of Daniel 2. The chapter's prediction of four and only four (rather than five or six) political systems binding together the old Roman Empire (the area centered in the Middle East and around the Mediterranean Sea) is remarkable, given the number of conquerors who have sought to glue the thing back together. But no one has been able to make the iron stick to the clay (verse 43).

By its very nature Daniel 2 leaves no room for preterism, futurism, or idealism. It is plainly historicist, running from the time of Daniel to the Second Advent. More important, Daniel 2 sets the prophetic pattern for the prophecies of Daniel 7, 8, and 9, and 10-12.

By its very nature Daniel 2 is plainly historicist, running from the time of Daniel to the Second Advent. More important, Daniel 2 sets the prophetic pattern for the prophecies of Daniel 7, 8, and 9, and 10-12.

Historicism is not as much on the surface in the book of Revelation. Revelation 12 is its most obvious historicist treatment. It runs from the birth of the Christ child up to the end of time, when the dragon becomes angry with the woman and goes off to make war with the rest of her offspring, who keep the commandments of God (Rev. 12:17).

Before moving on, we should note that Revelation 12:17 not only informs us that at the end of time God will have a commandment-keeping people, but sets the stage for chapters 13 and 14, with chapter 13 expanding on the last-day dragon power of Revelation 12:17 and chapter 14 on the last-day woman of that verse, and both chapters dealing with the final conflict over the commandments and allegiance or worship. Then, in turn, chapters 15-19 build on the concepts introduced in Revelation 13 and 14. Thus the historicist flow of Revelation 12 sets the stage for the eschatological half of the book, with verse 17 presenting the big picture and chapters 13-19 progressively supplying the unfolding details.

Whereas in my questioning journey I concluded that there is no ground for moving away from the obvious, on the surface, historicism of Daniel 2 and the subsequent prophecies that build upon it, I should note that I did find one aspect of traditional Adventist interpretation less than satisfactory. For some reason Uriah Smith and those who followed his lead interpreted the feet and toes (and by extension the 10 horns of Daniel 7) that wouldn't stick together as being Europe. That, it seems to me, is a Eurocentric position that does not line up with the Holy Land focus of the book of Daniel.

That insight, however, merely strengthens the prophecy, since if Europe has found it more difficult to maintain unity than to bind iron to clay, the Bible lands and Mediterranean area with their powerful religious divisions have been infinitely more impossible to unite.

At any rate, I found the historicist framework of prophetic interpretation to be foundational in Scripture itself.

The Year-for-a-Day Principle

A second fruitful area for apocalyptic doubt has been the year-for-a-day principle. That topic has taken a major hit in some sectors of Adventism in the past 30 years.

But once again my doubts came to a screeching halt in the book of Daniel, especially in the ninth chapter. Part of the problem interpreters of that chapter face is that there is absolutely no way to get from the time of Persia in sixth-century B.C. to the coming of the "anointed . . . prince" (verse 25, RSV) or "Messiah the Prince" (KJV) or Christ in 69 literal weeks. For that reason among others, some Bible translations (even by scholars who generally do not believe in predictive prophecy and hold that someone penned the book of Daniel in the second century before Christ, rather than the

Some Bible translations (even by scholars who generally do not believe in predictive prophecy) have felt compelled to translate the 70 weeks of Daniel 9 as "weeks of years," even though the word "years" is not in the Hebrew.

sixth) have felt compelled to translate the 70 weeks of Daniel 9 as *"weeks of years,"* even though the word "years" is not in the Hebrew (see, for example, RSV on Daniel 9:24 and Moffatt on Daniel 9:24, 25, 26, 27). Even liberal commentaries have tended to interpret the 70 weeks as "weeks of years."[2]

They found themselves compelled to include "years" by the very logic of the text. It is the only way one can make sense out of the passage, irrespective of a person's view of predictive prophecy or the date of Daniel's composition. Of course, the text implies "weeks of years" even if one doesn't translate it that way because of the in-built day-for-a-year principle needed to span the period from Persia to Christ.

Revelation 10 and the Unsealing of Daniel

A third area that I began to question was the traditional Adventist interpretation of Revelation 10, which stipulated that the opening of the little book that was sweet in the mouth but bitter in the belly was the discovery of Daniel's time prophecies and the Great Disappointment.

Now I was aware of Miller's interpretation of his movement having opened the little book of Daniel, the prophecies of which were sweet in the mouth.[3] And I knew Ellen White's position that "the book that was sealed was not the book of Revelation, but that portion of the prophecy of Daniel which related to the last days. . . . When the book [of Daniel] was opened, the proclamation was made, 'Time shall be no longer.' (See Revelation 10:6.) The book of Daniel is now unsealed."[4]

Beyond that, I was aware that the sealed book of Revelation 5 and that of chapter 10 are not the same book, since the text labels them with two different Greek words. (But just because they are two distinct documents does not mean that the contents of the "big book" and the "little book" do not overlap in some of their eschatological content.)

It also is evident to anyone who reads Revelation 9:13-11:18 that the opening of the little book takes place between the sixth and seventh trumpets, and that the seventh trumpet signals the Second Advent (see Rev. 11:15; 10:6, 7).

But the traditional Adventist interpretation, I mused, seems a bit too clean to be true. It appeared to be a little too Adventist-centered and smacked too much of our agenda. Thus my ongoing investigation of Revelation 10.

One preliminary lead was the obvious relationship between Revelation 10:5, 6 and Daniel 12:7. Commentators generally have pointed to the fact that verses 5 and 6 are a citation from Daniel 12:7.[5]

But even more profitable was Daniel 12:4, in which we find a book sealed until the time of the end. Whereas in Revelation 10 we have a book unsealed at the end of time.

What really caught my eye was that Daniel notifies us of only two parts of his visions that were sealed:

1. The 1260-day prophecy (alternately, 42 months, or a time, two times, and half a time), which is "shut up and sealed until the time of the end" (Dan. 12:5-9).

2. The vision of the evenings and mornings of Daniel 8, "for it pertains to many days hence" (verse 26).

With that information in mind, I found Joyce Baldwin's remark in her volume of the Tyndale Old Testament Commentaries to be insightful: "The reason why Daniel was to keep his last two visions sealed was that they were not yet relevant (8:26; 12:9), at least not in all their detail."[6]

Of course, my Adventist-informed eyes had no difficulty linking the sealing of the vision of the evenings and mornings of Daniel 8:26 to the 2300 days of verse 14. And it is a correct linkage. The first 14 verses of Daniel 8 provide four prophetic symbols (verses 3, 5, 9, 14), which the angel Gabriel arrives to explain in verses 15-26. His explanation lets Daniel know that the vision will extend until "the time of the end" (verse 17; cf. verse 19), and then goes into a prophetic history lesson beginning with Media-Persia (verse 20) and Greece (verse 21) and extending up through the power (Rome) that would destroy Israel (verse 24) and stand up against the Prince of princes (verse 25), but finally notes that the 2300-day prophecy would be sealed, since its fulfillment "pertains to many days hence" (verse 26). Gabriel's explanation tells us that the prophecy of the 2300 days of Daniel 8:14 would not be unsealed until the time of the end (see verse 17). At that time, according to the traditional Adventist understanding of Revelation 10, it would be sweet in the mouth, but bitter in the belly.

Daniel notifies us of only two parts of his visions that were sealed.

By that point in my study of Revelation 10 in relation to Daniel my interest had definitely been aroused. But, I still said to myself, perhaps this is all too neat. What evidence in Revelation itself can I find that it was the book of Daniel that was opened? I didn't want to hear it from William Miller, Ellen White, or Adventist history.

I was hoping to find a good article correlating the book of Daniel with the opening of the little scroll in Revelation 10. But not discovering one, I did the obvious. I compared the two books myself. And at that point I fell into an ocean of richness in terms of textual evidence.

The first thing to hit me was that as soon as the little book of Revelation 10 is opened we find a virtual explosion of material coming from Daniel in the Apocalypse of John. Take the 1260 days, for example. Immediately after Revelation 10 the 1260 days become a central feature:

- 11:2—The court of the temple "is given over to the nations, and they will trample over the holy city for forty-two months."
- 11:3—"And I will grant my two witnesses power to prophesy for one thousand two hundred and sixty days."
- 12:6—"The woman fled into the wilderness . . . for one thousand two hundred and sixty days."
- 12:14—The woman flees from the serpent "into the wilderness . . . for a time, and times, and half a time."
- 13:5—The beast exercised "authority for forty-two months."

It is significant that not once does Revelation mention that time period until the little book is opened. And at that point it shows up everywhere.

That conclusion led me back to the book of Daniel and the first mention of the 1260-day prophecy: The little-horn power "[1] shall speak words against the Most High, and [2] shall wear out the saints of the Most High, and [3] shall think to change the times and the law; for they shall be [4] given into his hand for a time, two times, and half a time" (7:25).

As soon as the little book of Revelation 10 is opened we find a virtual explosion of material coming from Daniel in the Apocalypse of John.

Each of the four parts of that verse forms a piece of the drama in Revelation 11-14.

1. The speaking of "words against the Most High" turns up in Revelation 13:5, in which "the beast was given a mouth uttering haughty and blasphemous words" for 42 months (cf. verse 6).
2. The wearing out of the saints is reflected in Revelation 13:7, in which the beast "was allowed to make war on the saints and to conquer them."
3. The part about the attempt to change times and laws is answered in Revelation 12:17, 14:12, and 14:7, in which God predicted a restoration of the commandments, including the one dealing with time, at the end of history.
4. And we have already noted the centrality of the 1260 days (or "a time, two times, and half a time") in Revelation.

Truly when the little book of Revelation 10 opens, we find an explosion of Daniel in John's Apocalypse, indicating that the sealed prophecies of the little book of Daniel had indeed been opened. But we are not finished yet with ideas related to the unsealing of the 1260 days. For the sake of brevity I will list just some of them.

The restoring of dominion to Christ and the saints at the end of the judgment of Daniel 7:14, 27 surfaces in Revelation 11:15.

The 10 horns of Daniel 7:7 are resurrected in Revelation 12:3 and 13:1.

The sea beast of Revelation 13:1, 2 represents a composite of the beasts in Daniel 7:3-6.

The victorious Son of man picture of Daniel 7:13, 14 comes up again in Revelation 14:14.

The problem of who to worship treated in Daniel 3 is a central feature of Revelation 13 and 14, in which we find the choice between worshipping the beast and its image or the Creator God alluded to eight times.

There is probably more that can be said, but the point has been made. Immediately following the opening of the little book of Revelation 10 the symbols of Daniel related to the sealed 1260 days become omnipresent in Revelation 11-14, whereas that symbolism was absent before the unsealing.

At that point in my study I had no doubt concerning the opening of the 1260 days that had been sealed in Daniel 12:9. But what about the unsealing of the 2300-day prophecy of Daniel 8:14-26? Here the evidence is not as rich, but neither is it absent. That prophecy deals with the cleansing, restoration, or justification of the sanctuary. And in chapter 2 we saw that early Seventh-day Adventists viewed that passage in terms of Day of Atonement symbolism in relation to the second apartment of the heavenly sanctuary.

With those thoughts in mind, it is of interest that Revelation 11:1, 2 presents a judgment scene in which the temple, the altar, and the saints are "measured." Commentators have looked for the Old Testament background to that passage in such places as Zechariah 2:1-5 and Ezekiel 40-48, but, as Ken Strand points out, the only adequate Old Testament passage is the Day of Atonement description of Leviticus 16. "In that chapter," he writes, "there are four basic entities noted as having

Immediately following the opening of the little book of Revelation 10 the symbols of Daniel related to the sealed 1260 days become omnipresent in Revelation 11-14, whereas that symbolism was absent before the unsealing.

atonement made for them—the priests themselves, the sanctuary, the altar, and the congregation (see vss. 6, 11, 16-18). The priesthood would obviously be omitted in any NT parallel, for Christ as High Priest . . . would need no atonement for himself. It is striking, then, that the three other exact entities to be atoned for in Leviticus 16 are *precisely those three elements* to be 'measured' in Revelation 11:1.

"A commonality in the *order* or *sequence* of the three items is also noteworthy. In both cases, the movement is from sanctuary/temple *to* altar *to* worshippers."

Strand adds that "the ancient Day of Atonement was a sort of final day of 'measuring' within the Israelite cultic year. It had an aura of final judgment about it, for on that day separation was to take place."[7]

In addition to the Day of Atonement/measuring/judgment implications of Revelation 11 is the fact that the second apartment of the heavenly sanctuary is first opened in Revelation 11:19. Whereas the sanctuary is central to the book of Revelation, its first half features first-apartment symbolism, with the action shifting to the second apartment in Revelation 11:19.

Also interesting as we think of the implications of Daniel 8:14 is the fact that the judgment scenes regarding the saints and the little horn in Daniel 7 and 8 and Revelation 11:15-18 are fleshed out in Revelation 14-20. Along that line, it is significant that Revelation 14:7 signals the fact that the "hour of [God's] judgment has come."

By this time in my study of Revelation 10 as it relates to the sealed portions of Daniel I was becoming quite excited. At that point I moved beyond the sweet but bitter experience of opening the little book (Rev. 10:8-10) to Revelation 10:11, in which we discover that out of the bitter experience would come a new message that must go to the whole world. That message is echoed in Revelation 14:6, which also claims a message that must be given "to every nation and tribe and tongue and people."

From those linkages it seems to me that the relevance of the time prophecy of Daniel 8:14 for our day is not so much connected to anyone's personal salvation as it is a *historical anchor point* for the last-day message of Revelation 12:17-14:20 that God commanded His people to preach to the entire world before the Second Advent. Put slightly differently, the significance of Daniel 8:14 is that it is an anchor point in time for the beginning of a last-day message predicted in Revelation 10:11 after the bitter experience. The passage running from Revelation 11:1 to 14:20, especially Revelation 14:6-12, identifies that message.

The Meaning of Daniel 8:14

That conclusion brings me to my problem with Daniel 8:14. It seems safe to say that there is no text in the Bible for many Seventh-day Adventists that is more unpopular, especially among the sophisticated. Most problematic for many is the teaching that the investigative or pre-Advent judgment of the saints began in 1844.

And we should note that here indeed the traditional position has a problem that we should not minimize. But that problem is not one of dating the fulfillment, in spite of widespread doubts on that topic during the past 30 years. After all, Daniel 8:17-19 plainly states that the vision will be for the time of the end. And the linkage running from Daniel 12:4 through Daniel 8:26 and through Revelation 10 demands an end-time fulfillment.

Beyond that, conservative exegetes widely agree that the best date for beginning the 70-week prophecy of Daniel 9 is 457/458 B.C.[8] And historicist writers have rather consistently placed the fulfillment of the 2300 days between 1843 and 1847.[9]

The problem in our day is not that the validity of the arguments for the dating has changed. Rather,

The relevance of the time prophecy of Daniel 8:14 for our day is not so much connected to anyone's personal salvation as it is a historical anchor point for the last-day message of Revelation 12:17-14:20 that God commanded His people to preach to the entire world before the Second Advent.

it is the fact that historicism with its year-for-a-day principle of interpretation is out of fashion in spite of the obvious evidence in such places as Daniel 2 and 9. In the early twenty-first century Seventh-day Adventists remain almost isolated on an historicist island. And those futurists who are more than happy to apply the year/day principle to Daniel 9 to get Christ born at the right time refuse to make the logical leap to using the same principle in Daniel 8. Here these largely conservative interpreters join the more liberal preterists in pointing to Antiochus Epiphanes (d. 164 B.C.) as the fulfillment. But Antiochus is hardly "exceedingly great" (Dan. 8:9). Historically he was a wimp who quickly backed down when confronted by Rome. The Antiochus interpretation of Daniel 8 on the little horn is based on 1 Maccabees 1:1-10, 54, but Josephus's later explanation shares a fuller perspective. While seeing Antiochus as a partial fulfillment, he goes on to apply the prophecy to Rome, the real "desolator" of Israel.[10] Jesus' interpretation harmonized with that of Josephus when He placed "the abomination that causes desolation" (Matt. 24:15, NIV) in the future rather than in the past.

Some people are surprised when I say that I believe that prophecy was fulfilled in 1844. But there is no better date, even though I see no point in overly emphasizing the exact day, given the varied discussions on the Karaite calendar versus other possible dating schemes for the Day of Atonement.

Three times Daniel 7 plainly teaches a pre-Advent judgment.

Detractors will always attack what they perceive to be an argument's weakest point. The good news is that the big picture is clear. I have found that those who give up the 1840s dating usually don't supply an alternative. To the contrary, they just drop the time element and avoid the topic except to take potshots at the traditional understanding.

That thought brings me back to my real problem with the traditional understanding of Daniel 8:14, which has to do with what Adventism has done with the cleansing of the sanctuary. The time-honored view is that the cleansing is the investigative judgment of the saints.

But looking as hard as I can at the text, I find no investigative or pre-Advent judgment of the saints in that passage. What I do find is judgment on the little horn and a restoration, justification, and cleansing of the sanctuary in relation to that power at the end of the 2300 days.[11]

Here is a problem we ought to be aware of. Our answers have been too simple and have not been rooted in the text itself.

Nevertheless, that misunderstanding does not do away with a pre-Advent judgment of God's people beginning at the end of the 2300 days. Three times Daniel 7 plainly teaches a pre-Advent judgment.

1. Verses 9 and 10 have the pre-Advent judgment taking place in what appears to be the heavenly sanctuary/throne room. Following that judgment Christ receives dominion in verse 14.
2. Verse 22 has judgment being given in favor of the saints before they receive the kingdom.
3. And verses 26 and 27 have judgment against the little horn and for the saints being given simultaneously immediately prior to their receiving dominion.

Revelation 11:15-18, in which both Christ and the saints receive the kingdom in relation to judgment, reflects the Daniel 7 judgment scenes.

There is not the slightest doubt that Daniel 7 has a pre-Advent judgment of or for the saints. But some of us have so much baggage between our ears that it is difficult to focus our eyes on what the text actually says.

We should note that the judgment in Daniel 7 has two aspects:

1. It is against the little horn.
2. It is for the saints.

However, Daniel 8:14 mentions only the little horn. But since chapter 7 makes it plain that the little horn and the saints are judged at the same time, it is safe for us to conclude, through parallelism, that the pre-Advent judgment of *both* the little horn and the saints takes place at the end of the 2300 days.

Thus the Adventist understanding of a pre-Advent judgment is not the problem. Rather, it is the wrong use of Daniel 8:14 to prove a point that comes out of chapter 7.

Before moving away from Daniel 8:14, I need to note that it is misleading to say that the doctrine of a pre-Advent judgment in Daniel is unique to Seventh-day Adventism. After all, many others have found a pre-Advent judgment in Daniel 7. And many historicist exegetes down through history have pinpointed the 1840s as the time for the fulfillment of Daniel 8:14. The only thing unique about the Adventist position is the combining of those two conclusions.

> *The Adventist understanding of a pre-Advent judgment is not the problem. Rather, it is the wrong use of Daniel 8:14 to prove a point that comes out of chapter 7.*

The Pre-Advent Judgment

We are now ready to look at the problem of the pre-Advent judgment. Here is another topic that some of us Adventists have made hash out of.

There is no doubt about the centrality of a pre-Advent judgment in the three angels' messages. "Fear God and give him glory," we read in Revelation 14:7, "for the hour of his judgment has come."

The problem is not the pre-Advent judgment, but what we have done with it. Let me illustrate. One of my first visits to an Adventist church took place when I was an 18-year-old private in the Army. I went because I wanted to be with my girlfriend, but what I saw astounded me. Up front was an "old" woman (she was probably 40) who had an exceptionally long and bony finger that she utilized in pointing to each of us teenagers. Her message was that we had better lay awake at night and recall and confess each and every sin that we had ever committed, because if we missed one we would end up in the hot place. The judgment had begun, and who knew when our individual names might surface in it.

The tragedy of Adventism is that we made the pre-Advent judgment a fearful thing built upon a less-than-biblical understanding of sin, law, perfection, and even judgment itself. Spiritual insecurity and lack of biblical assurance was the result. "God is out to get you" was the message in the era of bony fingers.

> *The tragedy of Adventism is that we made the pre-Advent judgment a fearful thing built upon a less-than-biblical understanding of sin, law, perfection, and even judgment itself. Spiritual insecurity and lack of biblical assurance was the result. "God is out to get you" was the message in the era of bony fingers.*

But that is not the Bible teaching on the judgment. In Scripture the Judge is not against us or even neutral. The Judge is for us: God so loved the world that He gave His only Son for our salvation (John 3:16, 17). John 5:22 even tells us that "the Father judges no one, but has given all judgment to the Son."

The purpose of judgment in the Bible is not to keep people out of heaven, but to get as many in as possible. The big question is whether they have accepted the atoning sacrifice of Chirst and let it transform their hearts and minds (1 John 2:1, 2; Rom. 6:1-11; 12:1, 2; 2:4-7).

Here we need to point out that the judgment is not for God's information. Wake up! God knows each of our hearts already. But He has a problem. If all people have sinned (Rom. 3:23), and the wages of sin is death (Rom. 6:23), how can He give some what they don't deserve (grace) while giving others exactly what they do deserve (death)? The judgment and the books of judgment are not for God but for the rest of the universe. It has to do with the justification of God, which is foundational to His justification of those humans who have accepted Christ into their hearts and lives (Rom. 3:25, 26; 1 John 1:9). The big issue in many of the songs in

Revelation involves the justice of God in His judgments (see, e.g., Rev. 15:3, 4; 16:5, 7; 19:1, 2, 11). At the end of time God wants all His universe to be able to proclaim that salvation is His to bestow because "his judgments are true and just" (Rev. 19:1, 2) and "in righteousness he judges and makes war" at the Second Advent (verse 11). And to make sure that no doubts linger about His justice, He provides the saints with an opportunity for a final judg-

> *We need to point out that the judgment is not for God's information. Wake up! God knows each of our hearts already.*

mental review of His decisions before the obliteration of sin and sinners (Rev. 20:4, 9-15).[12]

Returning to God's judgment of Christians, the Bible pictures it as an event of joy and positive anticipation. Listen to Daniel and John on the topic.

1. Daniel 7:22—"Judgment was given for the saints of the Most High."
2. Daniel 7:26, 27—Judgment is against the little horn but for the saints, who receive the kingdom.
3. Revelation 6:10—It is the saints who cry out "how long" before the beginning of the judgment that will set things right.
4. Revelation 11:15-18—The reward of God's servants is tied to the judgment.
5. Revelation 14:6, 7—Judgment is linked with the good news or gospel.
6. Revelation 18:20—Judgment is for the saints and against Babylon.
7. Revelation 19:2—The judgments of God are viewed as the culmination of hope.

The tragedy is that traditional Adventism took a thing of joy and by combining it with less-than-biblical concepts of sin and perfection made it a thing of fear, dread, and insecurity. No wonder so many Adventists have hated the "investigative judgment."

That thought brings me to a presentation that I made on Ellen White's relationship to the Bible at the invitation of Brigham Young University, the seat of Mormon scholarship. That conference on religious authority hosted papers from Catholic, Orthodox, Mormon, and Protestant perspectives. In the question-and-answer session following my presentation a leading Protestant theologian observed that he and his colleagues weren't having any problem with the Adventist position on Ellen White—that their real difficulty was with the investigative judgment.

My response was the biblical view (as presented above) that the judgment is an event of joy to God's people. I then noted that I wanted to write a book titled *Judgment Is Gospel*. He responded that the Protestant community looked forward to such a book from an Adventist. Meanwhile, David Neff (editor of *Christianity Today* and a former Adventist pastor who had been deeply troubled by the traditional perspective) mentioned to me that he wished we would have taught the gospel perspective on judgment while he had still been with Adventism.

The Sanctuary

Related to Daniel 8:14 and the subject of the judgment is that of the sanctuary. Here I also developed some difficulties with how some of us Adventists have traditionally treated the topic. Take, for example, the Adventist interest in the geography of the heavenly sanctuary. Some Seventh-day Adventists I have met can look at the earthly tabernacle and report everything that is happening in heaven. They can, so to speak, not only tell us how many bricks and boards the heavenly sanctuary has, but what each brick and board means.

But I don't find that same perspective in the Bible. A case in point is Hebrews 9:4, in which the author places the altar of incense in the wrong apartment. He appears not to be all that concerned with the exact details, because he has more important things to talk about. The last part of Hebrews 9:5 points in that direction: "Of these things [the furniture of the tabernacle]," we read, "we cannot now speak in detail." The author of Hebrews undoubtedly could have said a great deal about the shape and structure of the earthly sanctuary, but that

Some Seventh-day Adventists I have met can look at the earthly tabernacle and report everything that is happening in heaven.

was not his purpose. He desires to rush on to the really important topic that will consume him from Hebrews 9:6 to 10:28—the ineffectiveness of the Levitical services in contrast to Christ's priestly ministry. In essence, Hebrews is not a lesson in the particulars of the heavenly sanctuary or its geography. Rather, the Epistle desires to teach its readers the all-sufficiency of Christ's once-for-all sacrifice and the efficacy of His heavenly ministry.[13]

Ellen White exhibits a similar lack of concern with the geography of the heavenly sanctuary when in *Early Writings* she places God's throne in the holy place. Her presentation in that passage seems to be more concerned with the shift of function in Christ's ministry than rigid geography.[14]

Now, I do not offer the illustrations from Hebrews and *Early Writings* to suggest that there are no geographical realities in the heavenly sanctuary or that they are unimportant. After all, we need to remember that John did see the opening of the second apartment in the heavenly temple near the end of time (Rev. 11:19). What the Hebrews and *Early Writings* illustrations do seem to imply is a flexibility not always reflected in the traditional Adventist interpretation. In other words, we humans may be more limited than we might wish in extrapolating heavenly knowledge from the particulars of an earthly model.

And here we have a serious issue. *All too often interpreters have reversed the polarities between the earthly and heavenly sanctuaries.* Thus instead of the earthly being a reflection of the heavenly, they have made the heavenly a reflection of the earthly. The upshot of that wrong lead is that some make unwarranted claims about the heavenly sanctuary based on details of the earthly.

We need to keep in mind that the earthly sanctuary was a copy of the heavenly (see Ex. 25:8, 9, 40; Heb. 8:1-5). In fact, Hebrews repeatedly claims that the earthly was a mere "shadow" of the heavenly (8:5; 10:1). And we all know that a shadow does not provide full knowledge. For example, I can tell certain things about my wife by her shadow, but her actual presence multiplies my data hundreds of times.

> **All too often interpreters have reversed the polarities between the earthly and heavenly sanctuaries.** *Thus instead of the earthly being a reflection of the heavenly, they have made the heavenly a reflection of the earthly.*

Not only is the earthly a mere shadow of the heavenly, but Hebrews 9:9 calls it a *parabole,* or parable ("figure," KJV; "symbolic," RSV), of the heavenly. Here is a point of the first magnitude in importance. We know that a parable teaches a main lesson and should not be exegeted in all its details. And so it is with the parable reflecting the shadow of the sanctuary. From it we can understand the broad outline of the plan of salvation and the two-phase ministry of Christ in the heavenly sanctuary, but we have entangled ourselves in useless and endless controversies whenever we have gone beyond our parabolic and shadowy knowledge.

We can afford to be humble about our knowledge of the heavenly. After all, Daniel pictures the throne room of God (the Most Holy Place) as having "a thousand thousands" waiting on God and "ten thousand times ten thousand" standing before Him (Dan. 7:10). Such dimensions dwarf human understanding.

Too inflexible of an application of our knowledge of the shadow can lead to some problematic conclusions. After all, Jesus is not pouring His blood on the altar of burnt offering. Nor is He spreading it on the horns of the altar. Beyond that, both the Bible and Ellen White are clear that Jesus upon His ascension was not locked in a little cubicle apart from the Father for 1,800 years. The New Testament repeatedly states that Jesus "sat down at the right hand" of God when He ascended (see Heb. 1:4; Acts 2:34). And Ellen White saw a throne in the holy place, indicating that same truth.[15] Adventism has faced endless snarls and challenges on its sanctuary doctrine because it has been tempted to overemphasize geography and exact parallels from what the Bible calls parabolic or shadowy knowledge.

Hebrews is neither for nor against the Adventist position. It has its own agenda of helping first-century Jewish Christians understand that they have something infinitely better in the ministry of Christ in the heavenlies than they had in the earthly Temple with all of its pomp and beauty and visibility.

Closely related to the unfortunate overemphasis on heavenly sanctuary geography by some Adventists has been the problem of at times acting as if the book of Hebrews is answering specific Adventist questions. Hebrews is neither for nor against the Adventist position. It has its own agenda of helping first-century Jewish Christians understand that they have something infinitely better in the ministry of Christ in the heavenlies than they had in the earthly Temple with all of its pomp and beauty and visibility.

With that purpose in mind, we need to beware of reading ideas into the text that are not there. It is important to realize that the book of Hebrews is no more interested in chronology than it is in geography. Thus, whereas Hebrews 9:23 states that heaven has things that need to be cleansed, it does not develop the full meaning of the heavenly cleansing and how it fits chronologically into God's plan. For that we need to study the ministry of the Levitical sanctuary, which is an example of Christ's ministry in heaven.

An equally serious problem is to read Hebrews 9:23-28 as if it were making a chronological statement about the Day of Atonement ministry. It is true that Hebrews 9:25 may be alluding to the Day of Atonement ministry, but its purpose is not chronological sequence. What Hebrews "is concerned with," William Johnsson points out, "is one supreme idea—*the all-sufficiency of His death*. [Hebrews] contrasts the Old Testament sacrifices with the one Superlative Sacrifice. To do this [Hebrews] takes the high point of the Old Testament religious year—Yom Kippur—and argues that even on this day the sacrifices did not resolve the sin problem. . . . That is, the highest point of the Old Testament cultic year could not purge sin away. Obviously, if the Day of Atonement services were inadequate, how much more all other sacrifices."[16]

Let me repeat my main points as I sum up. First, we create problems in sanctuary theology by placing undue emphasis on sanctuary geography. Second, we are heading in the wrong direction when we read Hebrews as if it were either propounding Adventist theology or arguing against it. Hebrews has its own agenda. Third, it is wrong-headed to project chronology into Hebrews 9. Most of Adventism's difficulty with its sanctuary theology center on those three areas.

Before moving away from the topic of the sanctuary, it is important to note that Hebrews does shed light on Adventist concerns even if it is not setting forth the Adventist position. Take, for example, Hebrews 9:23 with its emphasis on the fact that heaven really does have things that need cleansing.

Now, there is a concept that has raised eyebrows. What could possibly require cleansing in heaven? Uncleanness in heaven, William Lane writes, "has been dismissed as 'nonsense'" by many leading commentators. Yet, he responds, the wording in Hebrews 9:23 "clearly implies that the heavenly sanctuary had also become defiled by the sin of the people."[17]

It seems that Craig Koester in his *Anchor Bible* commentary has captured the only possible solution to the problem when he points out that Hebrews 9:23 can be understood typologically only in relation to the Levitical pattern. Thus "Levitical practice foreshadows Christ's cleansing of the heavenly tent at the turn of the ages."[18]

We Adventists have been all too willing to back away from clear Bible teachings in the face of some who consider them to be "nonsense." It's time to reverse that pattern. We are without doubt on solid ground when it comes to our sanctuary doctrine, but not when it comes to the way that some teach it.

As Adventists we can rejoice in the two-phase ministry of Christ in the heavenly sanctuary. And we need to preach more enthusiastically the centrality of the sanctuary to God's operations. On that point it is important to note that sanctuary symbolism is central to the book of Revelation, with the visions in the first half of the book related to the first apartment and the second half of the book featuring the second apartment, first opened in Revelation 11:19: "Then God's temple in heaven was opened, and the ark of his covenant was seen within his temple." That text has been important in both Adventist history and theology, since the ark contains the Ten Commandments, which come to the forefront between Revelation 12:17 and 14:12.

> *We Adventists have been all too willing to back away from clear Bible teachings in the face of some who consider them to be "nonsense." It's time to reverse that pattern. We are on solid ground in our sanctuary doctrine, but not in the way some teach it.*

Great Controversy Theology

One topic that I never did have a question about is the great controversy theology running from Revelation 12:17 to 14:20. I have had some problem understanding how it all might take place in the early-twenty-first-century world, but not in the basic biblical outline.

The placement of Revelation 12:17 at the end of the historical time line of chapter 12 sets the stage for chapters 13 and 14, with 13 treating the last-day dragon power and 14 the last-day woman, or church. Revelation 12:17 makes it plain that not only will the commandments of God be an issue at the end of time, but that conflict will rage over them, with pre-Advent history coming to a climax in Revelation 14:12: "Here is the patience of the saints: here are they that keep the commandments of God, and the faith of Jesus" (KJV).

Revelation 14:7 with its "worship him who made heaven and earth, the sea and the fountains of water" even specifies which command will be at issue. That allusion to Exodus 20:11 and Genesis 2:1-3 sets up the

Sabbath as an end-time controversial issue.

But what is at stake is more than merely a day. Revelation 14:7 indicates that the real issue is worship. And so it is in chapters 13 and 14, which raise the issue of worship eight times. Worship comes into especially sharp focus in the contrast drawn between those who worship the Creator God of the Sabbath in Revelation 14:7 and those who "worship the beast and its image" in verse 9. Here we note with interest that two of the Ten Commandments deal especially with worship. The second command treats false worship and is the topic of Revelation 13. The fourth commandment highlights true worship of God and lies at the center of chapter 14.

With the dominance of worship at the center of Revelation 13 and 14, it is clear that the day of worship in the great controversy as reflected in Revelation is merely an outward symbol of total allegiance and true dedication and worship. While the day is symbolic, it is not the central issue. After all, there will be plenty of Saturdaykeepers in hell. People can observe Saturday because it is the right day and yet be out of harmony with Christ. A person can truly observe Sabbath only through the power of the Holy Spirit as a transformed individual who loves God supremely and cares deeply for other people (see Matt. 22:36-40). If we are going to follow Revelation, we need to move beyond the day to matters of the heart, allegiance, and worship.

The good news about great controversy theology is that it is not something out of Ellen White's writings. It is all in the Bible. While its fulfillment may stretch our imaginations, there is given the condition of the world today, no place for doubt regarding the Bible's teaching on the topic.

The good news about great controversy theology is that it is not something out of Ellen White's writings. It is all in the Bible. While its fulfillment may stretch our imaginations, there is, given the condition of the world today, no place for doubt regarding the Bible's teaching on the topic.

The Remnant

Raising the issue of the great controversy in Revelation 12:17 also brings to mind the Adventist teaching on the remnant. Many have concluded on the basis of Revelation 12:17 and 14:6-12 that Seventh-day Adventism is the remnant church.

In this area there appears to be a conflict between the baptismal vow and the denomination's 28 fundamental beliefs. The baptismal vow speaks of Seventh-day Adventism as being the "remnant church," whereas the fundamental beliefs place the emphasis on a remnant message to be proclaimed to the world by that part of the end-time remnant already in the church. The controversy some years ago over titling Richard Schwarz's college textbook on Adventist history highlights the tension between the two positions. Some saw *Light Bearers From the Remnant* as the proper title, while others argued for *Light Bearers to the Remnant*. "To," reflecting the position of the denomination's fundamental beliefs, won out.[19]

> *The baptismal vow speaks of Seventh-day Adventism as being the "remnant church," whereas the fundamental beliefs place the emphasis on a remnant message to be proclaimed to the world by that part of the end-time remnant already in the church.*

I must admit that I am a Seventh-day Adventist today partly because we are the only denomination that I know of preaching the remnant message of Revelation 12:17-14:12—especially Revelation 14:6-12, the last three messages to be given to the world before the Second Advent at the end of chapter 14. I wish, however, that there were a hundred or more denominations preaching the remnant message of Revelation 14, rather than merely one.

I find myself an Adventist by conviction rather than choice. Seventh-day Adventist theology is not perfect, but it is the closest approximation to biblical truth that I can find.

God's eschatological remnant message found in the heart of the Apocalypse of John (Rev. 14:6-12) is
- an exciting biblical message.
- a message rooted in time (Rev. 10:10, 11; 12:17; 14:6-20).
- a message worth living and sacrificing for.
- a message that needs to go forth and be preached with vigor and sincerity.

May God help us to do just that.

[1] Kai Arasola, *The End of Historicism: Millerite Hermeneutic of Time Prophecies of the Old Testament* (Sigtuna, Sweden: Datem Publishing, 1990).

[2] See, e.g., James A. Montgomery, *The Book of Daniel*, International Critical Commentary (Edinburgh: T. & T. Clark, 1927), pp. 372, 373; Louis F. Hartman and Alexander A. Di Lella, *The Book of Daniel*, The Anchor Bible (Garden City, N.Y.: Doubleday, 1978), pp. 245, 250.

[3] William Miller, "Chronological Chart of the World," *Signs of the Times*, May 1, 1841, p. 20.

[4] Ellen G. White, *Selected Messages* (Washington, D.C.: Review and Herald, 1958), book 2, p. 105.

[5] See, e.g., G. K. Beale, *The Book of Revelation*, New International Greek Testament Commentary (Grand Rapids: Eerdmans, 1999), pp. 537-539; R. H. Charles, *The Revelation of St. John*, International Critical Commentary (Edinburgh: T. & T. Clark, 1920), vol. 1, p. 262.

[6] Joyce G. Baldwin, *Daniel*, Tyndale Old Testament Commentaries (Downers Grove, Ill.: InterVarsity Press, 1978), p. 206.

[7] Kenneth A. Strand, "An Overlooked Old-Testament Background to Revelation 11:1," *Andrews University Seminary Studies 22:* (Autumn 1984) 320-325. (Italics supplied.)

[8] See, e.g., Leon Wood, *A Commentary on Daniel* (Grand Rapids: Zondervan, 1973), p. 253; Charles Boutflower, *In and Around the Book of Daniel* (Grand Rapids: Zondervan n.d.,) p. 185; Stephen R. Miller, *Daniel*, New American Commentary (Nashville: Broadman and Holman, 1994), p. 266.

[9] L. E. Froom, *Prophetic Faith of Our Fathers*, vol. 4, p. 404.

[10] Josephus *Antiquities of the Jews* 10. 11. 7.

[11] Cf. William H. Shea, *Daniel 7-12*, Abundant Life Bible Amplifier (Boise, Idaho: Pacific Press, 1996), pp. 145, 152.

[12] See G. R. Knight, *The Cross of Christ*, pp. 103-121.

[13] See George R. Knight, *Exploring Hebrews* (Hagerstown, Md.: Review and Herald, 2003), pp. 152, 138, 139.

[14] Ellen G. White, *Early Writings* (Washington, D.C.: Review and Herald, 1945), pp. 54-57.

[15] *Ibid.*, p. 55.

[16] William G. Johnsson, *In Absolute Confidence: The Book of Hebrews Speaks to Our Day* (Nashville: Southern Pub. Assn., 1979), p. 116. (Italics supplied.) Cf. Knight, *Hebrews*, p. 168.

[17] William L. Lane, *Hebrews 9-13*, Word Biblical Commentary (Dallas: Word, 1991), p. 247.

[18] Craig R. Koester, *Hebrews*, The Anchor Bible (New York: Doubleday, 2001), p. 427.

[19] The 2000 edition of the book avoided the ongoing controversy by changing the title to *Light Bearers: A History of the Seventh-day Adventist Church*.

Chapter 4

The Fallacy of Straight-line Thinking and a Most Remarkable Prophecy

Well, some might say, it is plain what the Bible teaches about the great controversy, and it is clear that that particular eschatology did not come from Ellen White, as so many seem to believe. But we live in a civilized age in which few have the slightest interest in Sunday sacredness, let alone Sunday laws and all that nineteenth-century stuff. Let's get on with preaching the gospel and the genuinely important activities, such as feeding the hungry.

I resonate with such sentiments. That is, I resonate until I look closely at the flow of Bible prophecy and the course of eschatological, political, technological, and demographic history.

The Shaky Case for Straight-line Thinking

What most of us suffer from is straight-line thinking. Many of us in our younger years faced that sort of thing, when we dealt with non-Adventists, by quoting 2 Peter 3:3: "You must understand this, that scoffers will come in the last days with scoffing, . . . saying, 'Where is the promise of his coming? For ever since the fathers fell asleep, all things have continued as they were from the beginning of creation.'"

But now more and more of the scoffers are inside of Adventism. We are just plain fatigued in waiting for the "soon coming" of Jesus. For our day I would suggest that the significant passages are found in Revelation 18. Speaking of the fall of Babylon and world civilization, we read:

1. "In *one hour* has thy judgment come" (verse 10).
2. "In *one hour* all this wealth has been laid waste" (verse 17).
3. "In *one hour* she has been laid waste. . . . So shall Babylon the great city . . . be found no more" (verses 19-21).

The biblical picture is one not of gentle continuity into the future but of crisis and radical discontinuity in a rapid time frame that ushers in the final crisis. We have seen some illustrations of this in the not-too-distant past.

In October 1989, for example, I was a guest of the East German government, with permission to go anywhere I desired in that Communist country. No one could have predicted when the invitation had been extended that before I exited its armed gates the East German government itself would be collapsing, soon to be followed by the entire Soviet Bloc. For decades the Soviets had dominated our lives, and now "in one hour" it was all gone. One might have predicted Soviet Communism's fall—given the inadequacies of its system—but no one could have foretold the rapidity of its disappearance. I would like to suggest that the demise of the Soviet bloc is a historical type of what can happen at the end of time "in one hour"!

Another scenario deals with the September 11 crisis. All but the blindest individuals saw eschatological/apocalyptic possibilities in that event. People got religious everywhere. But what if September 11 had only been the beginning? What if September 12 had been Moscow, September 13 Beijing, September 14 London, September 15 São Paulo, and so on? The probability is that within 30 days we would have seen moves toward an international police state "to protect the people." All "in one hour" of earthly history.

Or what about the ecological threats that face Planet Earth on every hand as developed nations acceleratingly grasp and use more and more of everything and developing nations also decide to follow that path?

The biblical picture is not one of gentle continuity into the future but of crisis and radical discontinuity in a rapid time frame that ushers in the final crisis.

Especially watch the booming economies of China and India, with their combined 2.5 billion consumers. We have just begun to see the pressure that will come to bear on earth's resources. Jared Diamond argues in *Collapse: How Societies Choose to Fail or Succeed* that "there are many 'optimists' who argue that the world could support double its human population, and who consider only the increase in human numbers and not the average increase in per-capita impact. But I have not met anyone who seriously argues that the world could support 12 times its current impact, although an increase of that factor would result from all developing nation inhabitants adopting developed nation living standards."[1]

Or what would happen if a two-year drought hit the world's half dozen significant food exporters, or even the massively productive bread-basket that spreads over the North American Great Plains from Texas up through Canada? Who gets the food in times of shortage?

Beginning in the 1970s lifeboat ethics has sought to answer that question. The basic idea undergirding that social perspective is that "each rich country is a lifeboat that will survive only if it refuses to waste its limited resources on the hungry masses swimming in the water around it. If we eat together today, we will all starve together tomorrow."[2] The answer on how to deal with the problem is often discussed in terms of cooperation and compulsion. In times of significant crisis, the argument runs, it is those who play ball with those in power who will eat. It is not individual human rights that count, but the health of the social whole. Those who fail to co-operate are expendable. "Let too many people into a lifeboat," writes a Canadian university sociologist, "and all will sink. The same may be true of our spaceship called Earth."[3]

The international think tank called the Club of Rome sums up the eschatological potentials of the ecological/population crisis nicely when it reports that "the council wishes to correct three mistaken ideas about human rights. The first is that human rights concerns only individual freedoms—i.e., that they are not applicable to groups and communities. This idea has its roots in nineteenth-century liberalism and has been promoted by churches that emphasize 'individual salvation.' In reality, however, violations of human rights occur in entire sectors of society, and must be eliminated in the social context. The second mistaken idea is that the human rights question is 'nonpolitical.' The council believes that human rights are a political matter. . . . The third idea to be corrected is that standards of human rights apply only to 'others' while 'our' situation is different. *International cooperation is required to ensure the truly universal application of human rights standards.*"[4]

In short, contingency plans drawn up by secular groups and social scientists have long been in place to meet a crisis or crises of such a magnitude to divert the world from what appears to be a straight-line course into the future. A world community that is increasingly becoming interdependent along several axes awaits only a sufficient crisis to force it into some sort of survival mode.

And what might that crisis be? Come back and ask me during the millennium, and I will be smarter on the topic, but I do know that while most of us Adventists are hunkered down in our bunkers not saying much on the topic anymore, such information venders as *Newsweek* keep blowing a trumpet that sounds more and more apocalyptic. Here's a few items from recent issues:

- "The Truth About Denial" highlighted the global warming issue, suggesting that we may see a few degrees Centigrade temperature increase. That might not sound like much until we realize that the last ice age was only 5° C cooler than present levels.
- "A New Way of War" asked, "How do you stop foes who kill with devices built for the price of a pizza? Maybe the question is, *can* you stop them?"
- "State of Anxiety" dealt with the implications of the political disintegration of Pakistan, one of the world's nuclear powers. Bin Laden's mission would certainly become more feasible with a nuclear boost.
- And then there was the full-page advertisement of the History Channel's "2-hour television event" not-so-subtly titled "Life After People." "Welcome to Earth Population Zero" ran the accompanying blurb.

Not being a prophet, I don't know much about the future. But I am wise enough to realize that a multitude of present realities could jolt Planet Earth out of its course and create a worldwide social/political crisis.

A world community that is increasingly becoming interdependent along several axes awaits only a sufficient crisis to force it into some sort of survival mode.

Interestingly enough, the best books on eschatology are not even put out by Christian publishing houses. Paul Erlich's *Population Bomb* got me thinking in new directions in the 1960s. And more recently Jared Diamond's 2005 best-selling *Collapse: How Societies Choose to Fail or Succeed* has become required reading for those taking the pulse of current realities. Diamond, of course, hopes we can all become unselfish and learn to pull together before it's too late. To that wishful thought, I jotted in the margin of my copy: "Try *sin,* a universal fact that you have amply demonstrated in terms of selfishness that led to the fall of past cultures around the world and across time."

For those who would like to taste a non-Adventist Christian perspective, try Richard Swenson's *Hurtling Toward Oblivion: A Logical Argument for the End of the Age*, which deals with the "irreversibility of progress," the implications of the acceleration of the use of more and more of everything, the "fallenness of the world system," and "our collective yawn" in the face of it all.[5]

And for those who want to sample a specifically Adventist perspective, Marvin Moore's *Could It Really Happen? Revelation 13 in the Light of History and Current Events* sets forth an array of provocative data.[6]

Of course, I know that reading that kind of material has fallen out of fashion in an Adventism that is settling down to a comfortable earthly existence. But try it and you might find out why you are Adventist. Straight-line thinking might make us comfortable as we continue to pump up our 403Bs, 401Ks, and IRAs, but it is trumped by not only the Bible, but by the multiplying possibilities for total disaster in an era of the rapidly increasing potential of technology.

Jared Diamond's *Collapse* studies ancient and modern societies that have collapsed or are collapsing and notes the strange fact that societies often self-destruct at the height or apex of their prosperity, when all seems to be going well as they push the limits of their reserves. His conclusions line up nicely with Revelation's repeated "in *one hour*" (Rev. 18:10, 17, 19) proclamations.

> *Reading that kind of material has fallen out of fashion in an Adventism that is settling down to a comfortable earthly existence. But try it, and you might find out why you are Adventist.*

Not being a prophet, I don't know the shape of the future, but I do know that Jesus predicted the end of straight-line thinking. In Luke 21:26 He noted that men and women would be "fainting with fear" and foreboding because of what was "coming on the world."

And I do know of the finding of University of New York sociologist Michael Barkun that "disaster creates conditions peculiarly fitted to the rapid alteration of belief systems."[7] In other words, given a crisis of sufficient magnitude, people will act in unpredictable ways.

A case in point is that of the Japanese American children I attended school with immediately after World War II. They had spent their early years in an American "relocation center," which is merely a nice name for a concentration camp in democratic America.

In the wake of the Pearl Harbor panic "more than 110,000 people—

most of them native-born American citizens—who were never charged with crimes or given a hearing" found themselves imprisoned in American wartime concentration camps scattered from the California desert to Arkansas swamps.[8] Some years ago I had the privilege of visiting both the camp in Manzanar, California, and the infamous Nazi camp in Dachau. Interestingly enough, they had the same floor plan. But that wasn't the only similarity. In both cases the majority of inmates had been incarcerated merely for being "different."

All three branches of the federal government supported Japanese incarceration, and more than once the United States Supreme Court upheld the "exclusion order." Speaking for the Court in one case, "Justice Hugo Black acknowledged that in the absence of a war, this sort of curtailment of the civil rights of a single racial group would have been unconstitutional. He observed, however, that

Given a crisis of sufficient magnitude, people will act in unpredictable ways.

hardships are part of war and argued that the Japanese-Americans could be required to bear this one because national security required it."[9] That logic, in fact, is built into the preamble of the United States Constitution, which implies that the police powers of the state can come into play whenever something threatens the "general welfare" of the nation.

So much for liberty, even in the "land of the free." Given a sufficient crisis, things can change "in one hour."

The Japanese situation prompted constitutional historians Alfred Kelly and Winfred Harbison to conclude that "in future wars, no person belonging to a racial, religious, cultural, or political minority can be assured that community prejudice and bigotry will not express itself in a program of suppression justified as 'military necessity,' with resultant destruction of his basic civil rights as a member of a free society."[10]

The end of straight-line thinking and living awaits only a sufficient crisis and its accompanying panic. Along that vein we need to remember that the Austrian corporal whom we know as Adolf Hitler never gained power in the world's most literate nation through revolution or coup. To the contrary, people who were hungry and wanted "volks wagons" elected him.

In that sense 1930s Germany is a twentieth-century historical type of what can happen "in one hour." Strange things occur in the realm of significant crisis.

In the light of the Bible, history, and current trends, please don't tell me what can or cannot happen in the United States or anywhere else in the world. Straight-line thinking is a comfortable fiction rather than a reality in a fragile world.

Current Adventism reminds me of our good friend Sherlock Holmes and his sidekick Watson on a camping expedition. At midnight Sherlock jabs Watson awake, asking, "What do you see?"

The end of straight-line thinking and living awaits only a sufficient crisis and its accompanying panic.

Watson waxes eloquent about the beauty of the stars, the shape of the Big Dipper, and the magnitude of the Milky Way.

"You fool!" Sherlock shouts. "Someone has stolen the tent!"

That story reminds me of twenty-first-century Adventism. We have lost something of crucial importance, yet we sit gazing at the stars. But without that something we have a neutered message.

Ellen White's Most Remarkable Vision

That brings me to what I consider to be Ellen White's most remarkable prophecy. She made few actual prophecies regarding the future in her long ministry, but we find one of them in her first vision of December 1844.

"While I was praying at the family altar," she recalled, "the Holy Ghost fell upon me. . . . I raised my eyes, and saw a straight and narrow path, cast up high above the world. On this path the Advent people were traveling to the city, which was at the farther end of the path. They had a *bright light set up behind them at the beginning of the path, which an angel told me was the midnight cry [i.e., the prophetic understanding that led to a fulfillment of prophecy in October 1844].* This light shone all along the path and gave light for their feet so that they might not stumble. If they kept their eyes fixed on Jesus, who was just before them, leading them to the city, they were safe. But soon some grew weary, and said the city was a great way off. . . . *Others rashly denied the light behind them and said that it was not God that had led them* out so far. *The light behind them went out,* leaving their feet in perfect darkness, and *they stumbled* and lost sight of the mark and of Jesus *and fell off the path* down into the dark and wicked world below."[11]

Please catch that picture of December 1844. Those Adventists who would eventually become the American Evangelical Adventists and the Advent Christians would be at least 50,000 strong by the summer of

1845. And the spiritualizer Adventist movement would also consist of a large number of believers in early 1845. But both groups in different ways would reject their prophetic heritage and all but disappear during the next 160 years.[12]

By way of contrast, the Sabbatarian Adventist orientation had no members in 1845. That is, it did not exist and would not even begin to become visible until 1847/1848. But the Sabbatarians would build upon their prophetic heritage; be driven by the logic of Revelation 10:11, 14:6, and the apocalyptic vision to the far corners of the earth; and be approaching the 16 million membership mark in 2008.

At the present time two of the post-Millerite denominations have died, three are struggling to survive with a few thousand each, and the one that retained the apocalyptic heritage has prospered.

But it doesn't have to remain prosperous. I hope I never have to write a history of Seventh-day Adventism that echoes the latest histories of the Church of God (Seventh Day) and the Advent Christians. The final section of the 1973 history of the Church of God (Seventh Day) is titled "A Dying Church" and the essay's final words are from Christ's message to the church at Sardis: "It was alive, yet dead!"[13]

Similarly, the final section of Clyde Hewitt's impressive three-volume history of the Advent Christians is "*Should a Denomination Be*

At the present time two of the post-Millerite denominations have died, three are struggling to survive with a few thousand each, and the one that retained the apocalyptic heritage has prospered.

Told It's Dying?" And the book's concluding words are "*I devoutly hope some are listening. Amen!*"[14]

It might be helpful if some of us Seventh-day Adventists are listening also. "He that hath an ear, let him hear what the Spirit saith unto the churches" (Rev. 3:22, KJV).

In light of the trends among other post-Millerite Adventists, perhaps it is time to take Ellen White's statement on remembering our past history a bit more seriously: "In reviewing our past history, having traveled over every step of advance to our present standing, I can say, Praise God! As I see what the Lord has wrought, I am filled with astonishment, and with confidence in Christ as leader. We have nothing to fear for the future, except as we shall forget the way the Lord has led us, and His teaching in our past history."[15]

- The book of Revelation is a call to neutered Adventists, and those about to be neutered, to wake up before it is too late.
- The book of Revelation is a call to preach the message that made Adventism a worldwide movement.
- The book of Revelation is a call to join forces with the Lamblike Lion who desires to mount His white horse and bring an end to the mess we call world history.
- The book of Revelation is a personal call to you and to me to preach a neoapocalyptic message that utilizes nineteenth-century insights, but is consciously relevant to the twenty-first century.
- The book of Revelation is a call from Jesus to those who have ears to hear what the Spirit has to say to the church. May God help His church and its ministry. Amen!

> *The book of Revelation is a call to neutered Adventists and those about to be neutered to wake up before it is too late.*

---

[1] Jared Diamond, *Collapse: How Societies Choose to Fail or Succeed* (New York: Viking, 2005), p. 495.

[2] Ronald J. Sider, *Rich Christians in an Age of Hunger*, 4th ed. (Dallas: Word, 1997), p. 33.

[3] See Penelope ReVelle and Charles ReVelle, *The Environment: Issues and Choices for Society*, 2nd ed. (Boston: Willard Grant Press, 1984), pp. 146, 147.

[4] Ervin Laszlo et al., *Goals for Mankind: A Report to the Club of Rome on the New Horizons of Global Community* (New York: E. P. Dutton, 1977), p. 244. (Italics supplied.)

[5] Richard A. Swenson, *Hurtling Toward Oblivion: A Logical Argument for the End of the Age* (Colorado Springs, Col.: NavPress, 1999).

[6] Marvin Moore, *Could It Really Happen? Revelation 13 in the Light of History and Current Events* (Boise, Idaho: Pacific Press, 2007).

[7] Michael Barkun, *Disasters and the Millennium* (New Haven, Conn.: Yale University Press, 1974), p. 113. Cited in Moore, p. 239.

[8] Peter Irons, *A People's History of the Supreme Court* (New York: Viking, 1999), p. 349. See also Roger Daniels, *Prisoners Without Trial: Japanese Americans in World War II* (New York: Hill and Wang, 1993).

[9] Kermit L. Hall, ed., *The Oxford Companion to the Supreme Court of the United States* (New York: Oxford University Press, 1992), pp. 944, 945.

[10] Alfred H. Kelly and Winfred A. Harbison, *The American Constitution: Its Origins and Development* (New York: W. W. Norton, 1948), vol. 2, p. 822; cf. Daniels, pp. 107-114.

[11] E. G. White, *Early Writings*, pp. 14, 15. (Italics supplied.)

[12] For the dynamics of the decline of the Millerite denominations, see G. R. Knight,

Millennial Fever, pp. 327-339.

[13] Richard C. Nickels, *A History of the Seventh Day Church of God* (n.p., 1973).

[14] Clyde E. Hewitt, *Devotion and Development* (Charlotte, N.C.: Venture Books, 1990), pp. 367, 373. (Italics Supplied.)

[15] Ellen G. White, *Life Sketches of Ellen G. White* (Mountain View, Calif.: Pacific Press, 1915), p. 196.

Chapter 5

Living the Apocalyptic Vision in the Twenty-first Century

The first four chapters have presented the apocalyptic vision from the perspective of the book of Revelation. That viewpoint is one of the onward current of history as the great controversy works itself out in the conflict between good and evil, climaxing with the coming of Jesus in the clouds of heaven and the setting up of His everlasting kingdom.

It is important to recognize that Revelation's overview is only one aspect of New Testament apocalyptic. A second appears in the Synoptic gospels (Matt. 24; 25; Mark 13; Luke 21).

The Synoptic Apocalyptic

The synoptic apocalyptic has a different flow from the one in Revelation. Whereas each synoptic presentation begins with a description of what have been seen as "signs of the times," each ends with the counsel to watch and be ready because no one really knows when the end will come. Even the function of the signs, given the fact that most of them deal with events that repeat themselves throughout history, is not so much to tell us *when* the end will occur as to alert us to the fact that we must *live in a state of continual expectancy* as we look forward to the Second Advent, because no one knows "that day and hour" except the Father (Matt. 24:36).

The function of the first 41 verses of Matthew 24 is to develop in true believers an awareness of the Advent and to set them up for the teachings of Matthew 24:42-25:46, in which Jesus repeatedly urges them to watch and be prepared for history's climactic event.

The five parables from Matthew 24:42 up through the end of chapter 25 reveal what needs to take place in the lives of believers as they await their Lord. That is, *the passage running from Matthew 24:42 to 25:46 (and* the parallels in Mark and Luke) *informs us about how to live the apocalyptic vision in daily life.*

Before examining the progression that runs through the parables, we should note that an undercurrent appears in all of them—that the return would be:

- "delayed" (Matt. 24:48).
- "delayed" (Matt. 25:5).
- "a long time" in the future (verse 19).

And it has been a long time. Jesus knew what He was talking about.

The issue that Christ needed to deal with in the face of the discouraging and faith-threatening aspects of the delay had to do with the attitudes and daily lives of His followers in the long interim between His ascension and His second advent.

With verse 42 we come to the practical outcome of what has gone before in Matthew 24. If no one knows the time of the Advent except the Father (verse 36), then it behooves Christians to "watch," because they have no idea at what hour their Lord will return (verse 42).

The passage running from Matthew 24:42 to 25:46 (and the parallels in Mark and Luke) informs us about how to live the apocalyptic vision in daily life.

Then in verse 43 Jesus gives a short parable urging His followers to be constantly expectant. They are to be as alert as a householder who anticipates that thieves will break into his house. A constant state of watchfulness and readiness for the Lord's return is the message of this short parable. After all, "the Son of Man will come at an hour when you do not expect him" (verse 44, NIV). It is an interesting fact that throughout history the time when Christ is least expected to return is always "today."

William Barclay relates the parable of three apprentice devils sent to earth to complete their training. Each presented his plan to Satan for the ruination of humanity. The first proposed to tell people that there was no God. Satan replied that that would not delude many, since most have a gut feeling to the contrary. The second said he would proclaim that there was no hell. Satan rejected this tactic also, since most people have a sense that sin will receive its just deserts. "The third said, 'I will tell men that there is no hurry.' 'Go,' said Satan, 'and you will ruin men by the thousand.'"[1]

The most dangerous delusion is that time will go on indefinitely. "Tomorrow" can be a dangerous word. It is against this attitude that Christ warns us in the first of His five parables on watchfulness and readiness.

The second parable (verses 45-51) continues the theme of urgency and watchfulness, but with several added nuances. This parable stresses that Christians have duties and ethical responsibilities as they wait and watch. Their waiting is not to be done in idleness. Also in this story, the householder's return gets delayed for reasons of which the servants know nothing.

Unfortunately, delay can lead to bad behavior. Since the servants are on their own in an uncertain situation, one of them allows his baser passions to rise to the surface. He begins being unkind to others and living a loose life, thinking that he has plenty of time.

> *The most dangerous delusion is that time will go on indefinitely. Tomorrow can be a dangerous word. It is against this attitude that Christ warns us in the first of His five parables on watchfulness and readiness.*

But at that point Jesus reiterates the lesson of the first parable: "The master of that servant will come on a day when he does not expect him and at an hour he is not aware of" (verse 50, NIV). Then in verse 51 Jesus gives an added lesson—one that will surface again in the conclusions of the fourth and fifth parables (Matt. 25:30, 46). Unfaithful servants will lose their heavenly reward and will receive, instead, the same reward as the unfaithful Jews (Matt. 8:12), wicked people in general (Matt. 13:42, 50), and the scribes and Pharisees (Matt. 23:13, 15, 23, 25, 27, 29). Thus He drives home the concept of faithfulness and watchfulness in a more complete way than in the first parable.

The third parable (Matt. 25:1-13) carries on the theme of waiting in watchful expectation begun in the first two, but once again Jesus increases the complexity of the message. The scene of the parable is a Palestinian wedding—a ceremony that was typically a drawn-out affair lasting for a week or more. Weddings involved the entire community, and, unlike Western custom, the newlyweds did not go on a honeymoon. Rather, they stayed at home and kept open house.

Even though the parable of the 10 virgins has a Palestinian wedding feast as its backdrop, it is not necessary to understand all the ancient wedding customs to catch the major lessons of the story. However, one detail of crucial importance is that Jesus, as in Matthew 9:15, is the bridegroom. That in itself is a bold claim, since the Old Testament frequently describes God (rather than the Messiah) as the bridegroom and Israel as the bride (see, for example, Isa. 54:4, 5; Jer. 2:2; Hosea 1-3).

Beyond the coming of the Bridegroom, the emphasis of the parable is on the 10 virgins and their lamps (verse 2). In fact, the primary focus is really on the division between the virgins. The parable describes five as wise and five as foolish. The preparation they have made for the coming of the Bridegroom determines the difference between the two groups. All have lamps, but only half of them have brought sufficient oil.

Note that all 10 are outwardly Christians, for all 10 await the coming of the Bridegroom. Also remember that all 10 become drowsy and fall asleep (verse 5). Thus we are not dealing in this parable with believers and nonbelievers. All claim to be believers.

A major point in the parable is that the Bridegroom is "a long time in coming" (verse 5, NIV). That is why the virgins all sleep. Earthly necessities go on, even while Christ's followers await His return. No one can exist in a constant state of high-pitched alert. The theme of Christ's delayed return has already appeared in Matthew 24:48, and it will show up a third time in Matthew 25:19. The delay was undoubtedly already becoming a problem for some believers when Matthew wrote his Gospel in the third or so decade after Jesus' ascension.

The difference between the wise and foolish believers is not whether they sleep. They all do, But not all have prepared for the summons. Some have left their preparation to the last minute, when it is too late.

The difference between the wise and foolish believers, as we observed above, is not whether they sleep. They all do. But not all have prepared for the summons. Some have left their preparation to the last minute, when it is too late. Jesus says that they pay deeply for their neglect. The "door was shut" (Matt. 25:10), their probation has closed (see also Rev. 22:10, 11), and they miss the great "wedding supper of the Lamb" that takes place at the Second Advent (Matt. 25:10-12; Rev. 19:9).

Matthew 13:25 presents the moral of the story: "Watch therefore, for you know neither the day nor the hour." That moral, of course, has also been the undergirding rationale of the first two parables in the series. But this one adds the crucial insight that no individual can rely on another person's preparedness. In the judgment of God we each stand as individuals.

We should point out that the parable of the virgins does not indicate how we are to prepare for the Bridegroom's coming. That will be the topic of the final two parables.

The parable of the talents (verses 14-30), in common with the three preceding parables, continues to stress being ready for the Master's return. But it seeks to deal with a question previously not answered: What is readiness?

The meaning of readiness is the contribution of the story of the talents. The story line is quite simple. A man (Christ) goes away and gives talents (large units of money) to each of his servants. To one, he gives five; to another, two; and to the last, one talent.

The first two put their talents to work and increase their master's investment, but the third merely buries his in the ground for safekeeping. In the ancient world burying money wasn't such a bad idea if one desired only security. Of course, a person needed to remember where it was buried. The practice of burying valuables undergirded the parable of the hidden treasure in Matthew 13:44.

Readiness for the return of Christ does not mean passively waiting for the event. Rather, readiness is responsible activity that produces results for the kingdom of heaven—results that the Master can see and approve of.

But the master desires more than security from his investment—he expects the talents to be used for profit. This becomes evident when, "after a *long time*" (note the similarity on this point to the previous two parables—Matt. 24:48; 25:5), the master returns and demands an accounting to determine the faithfulness of his servants in his absence (verse 19).

In the judgment scene that follows he rewards the two servants who have been faithful in meeting their responsibilities during his absence, but he punishes the one who did nothing even though he knew the master expected him to do something with the talent (verse 24). The irresponsible servant not only receives no reward, but what he has gets taken away from him. In the opinion of the master, he fails to qualify for entry into the kingdom (verses 28-30).

The lesson is clear. Readiness for the return of Christ does not mean passively waiting for the event. Rather, readiness is responsible activity that produces results for the kingdom of heaven—results that the Master can see and approve of.

We also learn from this parable that God doesn't expect the same results from everybody. Christians have varying levels of ability (verse 15). However, it is not the amount of a person's ability that the judgment evaluates, but whether he or she has put to use the full range of abilities that God has given. People are not equal in ability, but they can be equal in effort. God expects good interest on His investment from each of us.

Another lesson from the parable of the talents is that faithful people are "rewarded, not with a well-endowed pension, but with even greater responsibility."[2] Greatness based on service (Matt. 20:26-28) will continue into the age to come. It is an eternal principle of the kingdom of heaven. Ellen White captures the concept nicely when she writes that true education "prepares the student for the joy of service in this world and for the higher joy of wider service in the world to come."[3]

The parable of the sheep and the goats (which is technically more of an apocalyptic judgment scene than a parable) brings the judgment theme that began in Matthew 23 to a climax. It also completes Jesus' developing teaching on readiness. Whereas the first three parables in the present sequence placed the emphasis on watching (Matt. 24:42-25:13), and the fourth stressed working while watching (Matt. 25:14-30), this one (verses 31-46) is explicit as to the essential nature of that working.

The story of the sheep and goats is a vivid word picture of the final separation that will take place when Jesus comes in the clouds of heaven. It is a picture that allows for no middle ground or any second chances. One is either a sheep (a standard Old Testament symbol for God's people) or a goat. One is either assigned to the right (the symbol of favor) or the left (the symbol of disfavor). There is no middle ground. Nor is the decision of the judgment open to appeal. The scene is one of finality. Those individuals failing to utilize the waiting and watching time appropriately before the Second Advent are eternally lost from the kingdom (verse 46).

A crucial element in the parable is that of surprise. Both the sheep and the goats are startled at the king's verdict in their particular cases. Both groups question that verdict (verses 37-39, 44).

The reason for the surprise stems from the false interpretation of true religion (see also James 1:27; Rom. 13:8-10) held by most people. The average person sees the heart of true religion as believing in right doctrines or as practicing certain ritual and lifestyle duties.

But that is not the biblical position. In one of the great Old Testament texts God says through Micah that what He requires of His children is not outward behavior or ritual obedience but "to act justly and to love mercy and to walk humbly with your God" (Micah 6:6-8, NIV). Jesus has already quoted that text three times in Matthew (9:13; 12:7; 23:23), each time in the context of verses dealing with a false understanding of true religion. And the rest of the New Testament picks up on that same theme. Thus James can write: "Religion that God our Father accepts as pure and faultless is this: to look after orphans and widows in their distress and to keep oneself from being polluted by the world" (James 1:27, NIV). And Paul can declare that "he who loves his fellowman has fulfilled the law" (Rom. 13:8-10, NIV; see also Gal. 5:14).

> *A crucial element in the parable is that of surprise. Both the sheep and the goats are startled at the king's verdict in their particular cases. Both groups question that verdict. The reason for the surprise stems from the false interpretation of true religion.*

Nor has the first Gospel been silent on the topic of true religion and its rewards. Jesus put it most plainly when He claimed that "if anyone gives even a cup of cold water to one of these little ones because he is my disciple, I tell you the truth, he will certainly not lose his reward" (Matt. 10:42, NIV). Again, He noted that one can sum up the two great commandments as love to God and to neighbor (Matt. 22:36-40); He defined perfection in terms of being merciful to one's enemies (Matt. 5:43-48; Luke 6:36); and He explicitly told the behaviorally oriented rich young ruler that if he would be perfect, he should sell his "possessions and give to the poor." His reward would be treasure in heaven (Matt. 19:21, NIV).

These teachings come to a climactic point in Matthew 25:31-46. Here, Jesus sets forth the standard of judgment in unequaled clarity. People are not asked what they believe or whether they have kept the

Sabbath, paid tithe, or taken good care of their health. While those things are important, one can practice them rigorously and still be totally lost (Matt. 23:23, 24). The real issue of the judgment is whether individuals have shown tangible love to their neighbors.

While that point is crystal clear in the first Gospel, Ellen White sums it up nicely. Commenting on Matthew 25:31-46, she writes that Jesus "pictured to His disciples the scene of the great judgment day. And He represented its decision as turning upon one point. When the nations are gathered before Him, there will be but two classes, and their eternal destiny will be determined by what they have done or have neglected to do for Him in the person of the poor and the suffering."[4]

Some have held that verses 31 to 46 teach salvation by works, but this is not the case. The passage speaks to the standard of the last judgment rather than to how one is saved. Underlying the entire first Gospel is the assumption that Christ paid the penalty for sin in His great mission of saving His people from their sin (Matt. 20:28; 1:21). The point in verses 31 to 46 is the tangible evidence as to whether an individual has been saved. If people have been saved, their lives will produce evidence that they have internalized the grace and love of God by their willingness to pass on His gifts to others. Thus Joachim Jeremias can write that "at the Last Judgment God will look for faith that has been lived out."[5] In like manner, Leon Morris tells us that "we must bear in mind that it is common to the whole scriptural picture that we are saved by grace and judged by works. . . . The works we do are the evidence either of the grace of God at work in us or of our rejection of that grace."[6]

If people have been saved, their lives will produce evidence that they have internalized the grace and love of God by their willingness to pass on His gifts to others.

An important lesson from the story of the sheep and goats is that the works that really count are simple and uncalculating. They are as simple as feeding the poor and visiting the sick. And they are uncalculating in the sense that those who perform them do not do so to heap up merit but because the love of God exists in their hearts and naturally overflows to others. Helpfulness and mercy have become natural for them. They have internalized the love of God, and it shows up in their daily lives, even though they are not conscious of that virtue.

On the other hand, the whole attitude of those deemed to be goats is that *if* they had known the sick and poor were important persons, they would have been the first to help them. They have had their gaze on prestige, reward, and recognition, and have failed to internalize the love of God. Thus they have missed the thing in religion that really counts. Their religion is actually a form of disguised selfishness.

To all such followers, Jesus says: "I do not know you" (Matt. 25:12). "Not everyone who says to me, 'Lord, Lord,' will enter the kingdom of heaven, but only he who *does* the will of my Father who is in heaven. Many will say to me on that day, 'Lord, Lord, did we not prophesy in your name, and in your name drive out demons and perform many miracles?' Then I will tell them plainly, 'I never knew you. Away from me, you evildoers'" (Matt. 7:21-23, NIV).

> *It is the unconscious internalization of God's love and its expression in daily life that is the one essential qualification for the kingdom of heaven. Such people have begun to live the principle of servanthood and greatness.*

It is the unconscious internalization of God's love and its expression in daily life that is the one essential qualification for the kingdom of heaven. Such people have begun to live the principle of servanthood and greatness that has come up again and again in Matthew's Gospel. Such people are safe to save for eternity because they have internalized the principle of love, *the* principle of the kingdom. And such people have developed through grace that "righteousness [which] exceeds that of the scribes and Pharisees." Thus they are prepared to "enter the kingdom of heaven" (Matt. 5:20).[7]

Balanced Apocalyptic Living

With the teaching of the synoptic apocalyptic in mind it is little wonder that down through Seventh-day Adventism's history some in the face of the delayed eschaton have been tempted to turn away from preaching the apocalyptic in Revelation and toward the synoptic version. Preaching Revelation in its apocalyptic flow was great for the nineteenth century, the idea runs, but it's out-of-date today. We need to get real, be relevant, and follow the example of Jesus in social justice, feeding the poor, and so on. That is the way to be meaningful in the twenty-first century.

There are only three problems with that solution as the primary mission of the church. The first and most significant is that Jesus rejected it. While He did much for the poor and suffering throughout His ministry, He realized that the world's problems would never be solved in that way. To follow the social justice route, points out Ravi Zacharias, is to "misread the script" of the New Testament.[8]

The best example of Jesus' position is the feeding of the 5,000, at which time the impressed populace moved to "take him by force to make him king" (John 6:15). They remembered that Moses, the great deliverer, gave their "fathers . . . manna in the wilderness" (verse 31). Here clearly was a second Moses—a second deliverer—another prophet (verse 14; Deut. 18:18), who like Moses could supply bread from heaven. Thus the move to make Him king. That possibility swept even the disciples along with it. Matthew tells us that Jesus had to "make" them get into the boat to start their homeward journey, while He dismissed the crowds (Matt. 14:22). For Jesus, the feed-the-poor route to the kingdom was the ultimate temptation. After all, He could indeed create bread out of "stones" (see Matt. 4:3, 4), and a people whose lives were all too often dominated by hunger had been impressed—so impressed that they were ready to set up the kingdom on the spot.

While Jesus did much for the poor and suffering throughout His ministry, He realized that the world's problems would never be solved in that way.

Here was temptation on the first order. *"Build the Kingdom, it suggests, on bread. Make it the first point of your programme to abolish hunger."*[9] *Such a thing is a truly relevant ministry. But it was a principal route to ministry that Jesus forcefully rejected* in both John 6 and Matthew 4. His primary avenue to ministry aimed at lifting his "listeners from their barren, food-dominated existence to the recognition of the supreme hunger of life that could only be filled by different bread. . . . He wanted to meet a greater hunger,"[10] the hunger of the human soul and the need of ultimate redemption. Thus, while He continued to feed the poor and point out the need for social justice, *Jesus' principal focus was the "irrelevant" one of the radical cross and the preaching of the gospel of full redemption from a world of sin.*

It is in line with that focus that we come to the second problem with the feeding-the-poor route to the kingdom, which is that it was Christ Himself who commissioned the preaching of the three angels' messages of Revelation 14 right before the Second Advent. It was Jesus who revealed Himself to John (Rev. 1:1-3) and who sends the three angels with their "eternal gospel" messages for the whole world (Rev. 14:6). Part of that good news is that "the hour of his judgment has come" (verse 7), sin's reign is finished, and God will soon come to rescue His people from this world of sickness, sorrow, death, and hunger (Rev. 14:14-20; 19; 21:1-4). Jesus' solution transcended that of patching our broken world through social tinkering, as good and praiseworthy as such action might be. To seek to separate the Christ of the synoptic apocalypse from the one in Revelation is a serious mistake. Both messages are from Him.

A third problem for Adventists in the take-care-of-the-poor-and-suffering as the primary apocalyptic program of the denomination is that Ellen White advised against it in no uncertain terms. The late nineteenth century saw J. H. Kellogg begin a very relevant and successful social justice movement for the poor and the outcasts. While Ellen White had no doubt that "this in itself is a good work" and that "the Lord has a work to be done for the outcasts," she was adamant that Adventist energies and money should not be "swallowed up in doing a work which the world would do largely." "But," she continued on, "the world will not do the work which God has committed to His people."[11] On another occasion she pointed out that the Salvation Army was doing a good work, but that Adventists were not to make that their primary focus. Rather, "the Lord has marked out our way of working. . . . The truth for this time is to be proclaimed."[12] And for her that truth was the messages of the three angels of Revelation 14. Ellen White never tired of reminding Seventh-day Adventists that many other people had a burden for social justice and a ministry to the poor and hungry, but that no

Jesus' solution transcended that of patching our broken world through social tinkering, as good and praiseworthy as such action might be. To seek to separate the Christ of the synoptic apocalypse from the one in Revelation is a serious mistake. Both messages are from Him.

one else was preaching God's last apocalyptic message. That preaching, she held, was God's special commission to Adventism.[13]

At this juncture we need to reemphasize that the apocalyptic vision in Revelation and the synoptic apocalypse are not in opposition to each other. To the contrary, they are complementary, with each having its proper place as illustrated in the ministry of Christ. That is, while He helped the outcasts and fed the poor, His primary ministry was the radical route of preaching a gospel that led to the cross. That same balance appears in the commission to Adventism as God seeks to prepare the world for the kingdom culmination that Christ initiated 2,000 years ago. *The ultimate message of both the book of Revelation and the synoptic apocalypse is that the only real solution to poverty and injustice is the return of Jesus. It is that solution that makes the Adventist message truly relevant to a dying world.*

Well then, we need to ask, how shall we live and act as we prepare for the Advent? We find the answer in both apocalypses of the New Testament. In line with such passages as Matthew 25 on the sheep and the goats, we need to care for the hungry and visit the sick, *but* we also need to preach God's last-day apocalyptic message. The two go hand in hand. Both in proper balance are important.

Ellen White never tired of reminding Seventh-day Adventists that many others had a burden for social justice and a ministry to the poor and hungry, but that no one else was preaching God's last apocalyptic message. That preaching, she held, was God's special commission to Adventism.

Here we need to note that Adventists have too often expressed a wrongheaded approach to the apocalyptic vision that has emphasized what is wrong with other churches, fear-mongering, and—worst of all—a fixation on time. Have a Sunday law show up on the horizon, and Adventists get excited. But they all too often have failed to see that time is not where Christ placed the emphasis.

To the contrary, in Mark 13:34 and the parables in Matthew 24 and 25 Christ explicitly teaches that those waiting for His return must put their emphasis on being faithful servants. Being faithful servants while we wait and watch sums up the most important lesson that Jesus gave us regarding the Second Advent in the synoptic apocalypse.

That disappoints some of us, because we are more concerned about the time of the Advent than with being faithful. But Jesus wants us to take our minds off of that obsession and to live every day in such a way that we will be ready when He returns.

How should we act if we discovered that the Second Advent would occur today? John Wesley somewhere put it correctly when he said that if he had such information he would go on doing just what he did every day in preaching God's message and loving God's people.

And how should we act if we discovered that the Second Advent would occur today? John Wesley somewhere put it correctly when he said that if he had such information he would go on doing just what he did every day in preaching God's message and loving God's people.

William Barclay points out the bottom line of the practical lesson of the synoptic apocalypse. It means "that we must so live that it does not matter when He comes. It gives us the great task in life of making every day fit for Him to see, and being at any moment ready to meet Him face to face. *All life becomes a preparation to meet the King.*"[14]

---

[1] William Barclay, *The Gospel of Matthew*, 2nd ed., Daily Study Bible (Edinburgh: St. Andrew Press, 1958), vol. 2, pp. 350, 351.

[2] Eduard Schweizer, *The Good News According to Matthew,* trans. David E. Green, (Atlanta: John Knox, 1975), p. 471.

[3] Ellen G. White, *Education* (Boise, Idaho: Pacific Press, 1952), p. 13.

[4] White, *The Desire of Ages*, p. 637.

[5] Joachim Jeremias, *The Parables of Jesus*, 2nd rev. ed. (New York: Charles Scribner's Sons, 1972), p. 209.

[6] Leon Morris, *The Gospel According to Matthew,* Pillar New Testament Commentary (Grand Rapids: Eerdmans, 1992), p. 634.

[7] For a broader discussion of synoptic apocalyptic, see George R. Knight, *Matthew: The Gospel of the Kingdom,* Abundant Life Bible Amplifier (Boise, Idaho: Pacific Press, 1994), pp. 232-250; George R. Knight, *Exploring Mark* (Hagerstown, Md.: Review and Herald, 2004), pp. 240-252.

[8] Ravi Zacharias, *Jesus Among Other Gods: The Absolute Claims of the Christian Message* (Nashville: Thomas Nelson, 2000), p. 79.

[9] James Denney, *Jesus and the Gospel* (London: Hodder and Stoughton, 1908), p. 210. (Italics supplied.)

[10] Zacharias, p. 79.

[11] Ellen G. White, "The Work for This Time," manuscript 3, 1899; Ellen G. White to

Bro. and Sis. Irwin, Jan. 1, 1900.

[12] Ellen G. White, *Testimonies for the Church* (Mountain View, Calif.: Pacific Press, 1948), vol. 8, pp. 184, 185.

[13] For a broader treatment of these issues, see "Occupying Till He Comes: The Tension Between the Present and the Future" in George R. Knight, *If I Were the Devil: Seeing Through the Enemy's Smokescreen: Contemporary Challenges Facing Adventism* (Hagerstown, Md.: Review and Herald, 2007), pp. 251-269.

[14] William Barclay, *The Gospel of Mark*, 2nd ed., Daily Study Bible (Edinburgh: St. Andrew Press, 1956), p. 337. (Italics supplied.)

Chapter 6

A Glimpse of Neoapocalyptic and a Belated Foreword

And what is relevant for the twenty-first century? What is it that Planet Earth really needs?

Those questions are at the core of what Adventism is all about. But its clergy and laity are divided over the answer.

In the face of what seems to be an ever-delaying Second Advent, many Adventists, especially talented young ones, are searching for a relevant, meaningful message for the new century. The direction more and more of them are taking is toward feeding the poor and social justice. Those things, as I noted in chapter 5, are good and necessary, but from the biblical perspective we can in no way view them as the "most relevant" Christian activities to meet the needs of the world. Jesus, even though He cared for the outcasts and fed the poor, repeatedly turned away from the social justice path as the primary focus of His own ministry. His message at its core was that social engineering and Christian benevolence would never solve the world's problems.

The only sufficient and permanent answer to the vicious difficulties facing a lost world, Christ taught in both the Gospels and in the book of Revelation, would be His victorious return in the clouds of heaven. Therein is real hope. All else is Band-Aids.

And hope is what people need more than anything. It is the promise of hope for a hopeless world that has made the book of Revelation relevant for every age.

A Glimpse of Neoapocalyptic

Our times need to hear what we might think of as a neoapocalyptic message that brings hope in Christ not only as the saving Lamb of God but as the returning Lion of the tribe of Judah, who will not only feed the hungry but abolish hunger, and who will not only comfort the grieving but eradicate death. The world has not only suffered too long but continues to suffer in spite of humanity's best efforts. Neoapocalypticism is the preaching of the ultimate hope that puts all other hopes in the shade.

Those of us who have at times suffered under beastly preaching and fear a return to the "bad old days" need to remember that Bible-oriented apocalypticism is not an exercise in bashing other churches, or fear-mongering, or encouraging people to live from one period of eschatological excitement to the next.

To the contrary, neoapocalypticism centers on Christ from first to last, presents responsible daily living as the path of the faithful as they joyfully await their Lord from heaven, and realizes that there is nothing more relevant than the coming of Christ, who will restore all things to their rightful place.

Neoapocalypticism's motivational force is love rather than fear. Its focal point is the future rather than the past. But in pointing toward future promises, neoapocalypticism will not forget the past. To the contrary, it builds solidly upon

The world has not only suffered too long but continues to suffer in spite of humanity's best efforts. Neoapocalypticism is the preaching of the ultimate hope that puts all other hopes in the shade.

understandings of the Bible that have informed Christians throughout the centuries, but also employs twenty-first-century events and dynamics to explain the progress of history as it moves toward its inevitable climax. While it utilizes nineteenth-century insights, neoapocalypticism integrates them with current realities. Thus it is respectful of the past but willing to move beyond it.

Jesus the hope of the world is neoapocalypticism in a nutshell. All else flows out from Him.

The Christ of Revelation, of course, is still the Jesus of the Gospels who forever encourages each of us to choose life over death, love over selfishness, and God over Satan. The call of Christ throughout the New Testament is to worship God supremely. That summons will continue on into the neoapocalyptic future as the church continues the preaching of the everlasting gospel of the three angels' messages to all the earth.

Neoapocalypticism does not shy away from the great controversy scenario set forth in Revelation 12 through 14. Instead, it recognizes that the center of the struggle is not mere outward obedience but a heart relationship with the Creator God. Such a relationship leads to total allegiance in a worship that overflows into a daily life of love that is partially expressed in the keeping of all of God's commandments.

Jesus the hope of the world is neoapocalypticism in a nutshell. All else flows out from Him.

Thus neoapocalypticism does not put forth a message of legalism, but one of true worship that takes God at His word. After all, it is the Christ of the Revelation who forcefully claimed that at the end of time He would have a people who are

1. patiently waiting for His return.
2. keeping God's commandments while waiting.
3. maintaining a faith relationship with God through Him (Rev. 14:12).

Finally, neoapocalypticism uplifts its specifically Adventist insights and integrates them with those of evangelical Christianity. And in that combination we find the message that God commanded in Revelation 14 to be preached to all the world before the Advent. It is that message that blazes forth rays of hope for a suffering world. It is that message that the risen Christ of Revelation deems *most relevant* for our day.

A Belated Foreword

You may have noticed that this little book did not have a foreword or preface. The omission was by design. I wanted readers to get into the topic and reflect on it later.

The Apocalyptic Vision and the Neutering of Adventism is not a slow-paced "scholarly" book. Rather, it is a tract for the times and a wake-up call based on the gut-level feeling that Adventism is losing its way and the observation that many of its younger ministers and members have never even heard the apocalyptic vision, while many of its older ones question whether they can any longer believe it or preach it.

I first presented the core of the messages in this book at the evening sessions of the quinquennial ministerial council of the Pacific Union Conference in August 2007. The topic, as I had anticipated, divided the audience of nearly 800 clergy. The evaluation of the presenters at the end of the council rendered me two honors: My series was voted both the *most valuable* presentations in the convention and the *least valuable*, albeit by a five-to-one margin in favor of most valuable.*

That evaluation is of importance because it indicates a radically divided ministry (and probably laity) over the very issues that make us Adventists. But more important to me than the formal evaluation were the repeated statements of ministers of both the Pacific Union and the Australian Union (where I presented the series in February 2008) that they could finally preach the Adventist message with confidence, that they at last felt comfortable with teaching the pre-Advent judgment, and even that they were glad that they finally had seen the major parts of the apocalyptic package in context.

The Apocalyptic Vision and the Neutering of Adventism *is not a slow-paced "scholarly" book. Rather, it is a tract for the times and a wake-up call based on the gut-level feeling that Adventism is losing its way and the observation that many of its younger ministers and members have never even heard the apocalyptic vision, while many of its older ones question whether they can any longer believe it or preach it.*

My prayer is that God may help us preach and teach His apocalyptic message in its unneutered fullness and balance, and that we might have ears to "hear what the Spirit says to the churches" in John's great vision.

—George R. Knight
Rogue River, Oregon

---

* Gerry Chudleigh and Julie Masterson, "Ministerial Council Overflows," *Pacific Union Recorder*, December 2007, p. 31.

Lest We Forget ...

"We have nothing to fear for the future, except as we shall forget the way the Lord has led us, and His teaching in our past history."—Ellen G. White.

JAMES WHITE
Innovator and Overcomer

Gerald Wheeler explores James White's personality, family, theology, and entrepreneurship—and reveals how personality traits and events shaped White as a man and leader. 0-8280-1719-0.

3 WAYS TO SHOP

• Visit your local ABC
• Call 1-800-765-6955
• www.AdventistBookCenter.com

REVIEW AND HERALD ®
PUBLISHING ASSOCIATION
Since 1861 | www.reviewandherald.com

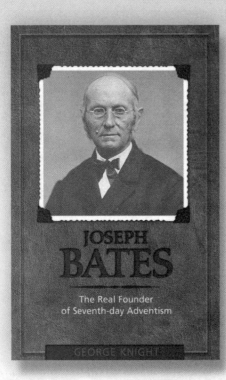

Lest We Forget...

"We have nothing to fear for the future, except as we shall forget the way the Lord has led us, and His teaching in our past history."—ELLEN G. WHITE.

JOSEPH BATES

The Real Founder of Seventh-day Adventism

George Knight sheds new light on the first theologian and real founder of the Adventist Church—a man who gave his estate to the Advent movement and spent the rest of his life in unpaid service to his King. 0-8280-1815-4.

3 WAYS TO SHOP

- Visit your local ABC
- Call 1-800-765-6955
- www.AdventistBookCenter.com

Lest We Forget...

"We have nothing to fear for the future, except as we shall forget the way the Lord has led us, and His teaching in our past history."—ELLEN G. WHITE.

W. W. PRESCOTT
Forgotten Giant of Adventism's Second Generation
Gilbert Valentine examines Prescott's impact on the church's educational system and how he helped reshape the church's theology and policies during a critical era.

E. J. WAGGONER
From the Physician of Good News to Agent of Division
Woodrow Whidden traces the life and public ministry of one of Adventism's most controversial pioneers—a man who received both stern rebuke and emphatic support from Ellen White and whose theological contributions have shaped, and divided, the Adventist Church. Hardcover, 368 pages.

3 WAYS TO SHOP
- Visit your local ABC
- Call 1-800-765-6955
- www.AdventistBookCenter.com

REVIEW AND HERALD®
PUBLISHING ASSOCIATION
Since 1861 | www.reviewandherald.com

Prices and availability subject to change. Prices higher in Canada.